Tolstoy

Principles for a New World Order

TOLSTOY

Principles for a New World Order

David Redfearn

SHEPHEARD-WALWYN

© 1992 David Redfearn

First published 1992 by
Shepheard-Walwyn (Publishers) Ltd
Suite 34, 26 Charing Cross Road
London WC2H 0DH

ISBN 0 85683 134 4

British Library Cataloguing-in-Publication Data
A catalogue record of this book is available
from the British Library

Typeset by The Wordfactory
Falmouth, Cornwall
Printed and bound in Great Britain by
BPCC Wheatons Ltd, Exeter

Contents

Acknowledgements

My thanks are due to Fred Harrison for prompting me to write the book and for his support until the task was completed.

I am also grateful to Shirley-Anne Hardy and Professor Robert V. Andelson for many helpful, detailed suggestions.

With my exposition of the philosophies of both Leo Tolstoy and Henry George, and my defence of them against misguided criticism, I think I can claim that these friends of mine are in agreement. When, however, I have gone beyond such exposition and such defence, and expressed opinions of my own, then I and I alone am responsible.

The two appendices, which constitute the full texts of Tolstoy's letters to the Tsar Nicholas II and to the Grand Duke Nikolay Mikhaylovich, are repoduced here by courtesy of the Athlone Press from *Tolstoy's Letters,* 1978, edited by R.F. Christian.

Finally, my thanks to my wife Kay, an admirier of Tolstoy, for all help and encouragement.

David Redfearn,
Eastbourne,
May 1991.

Foreword

IN many countries of the world there is a sustained interest in the personality and creativity of Leo Tolstoy, and especially in the moral philosophy on which he worked in his later years. Why is his work of value to us in the world of today? Because, on the one hand, the scientific and technical revolutions of this century have claimed priority over humanity and morality becasue, and, on the other, because aggressive consumerism has replaced the love of creative art.

Tolstoy had a profound understanding of the cultures of the world, in that he realised that all religions are based on one idea, the union of the people in love, and that all wisdom and morality have this as their aim. We can easily see the parallels between Tolstoy's appeal for dynamic love to overcome the unchecked forces of evil and the basic principles of the ancient Hindu philosophy of Ahimsa [never to inflict injury on sentient beings]. We can also compare his appeal with those of Laotze, Socrates and the Stoics, who taught that 'it is better to suffer injustice than to be the cause of it', and with Christ's injunction [Matthew v, 43]: 'Love your enemies ...'. Nevertheless, Tolstoy was critical of many attitudes of the Christian churches, and contrasted them with his own humanitarian values. Also, he was concerned with such cultural obligations as the strenuous and persistent search for truth, not only in the outside world but also within oneself.

Tolstoy lived out his humanitarian values and moral wisdom on his estate, Yasnaya Polyana, a place of pilgrimage from all over the globe. One witness to his lifestyle was Mahatma Gandhi, 'the son of the Indian people'. Tolstoy's confidence in reason and experiment led him to embody his vision of human morality and wisdom in a collection of extracts from great

vii

writers on which he worked systematically until his last years. It appeared in three variant editions under the titles of *A Circle of Reading* and *For Every Day,* but was never finished to his satisfaction. His followers' duty is now to complete and publish what he thought of as The Moral Wisdom of the World.

The important task that Tolstoy set himself was the freeing of the world from spiritual degeneration and evil; and he directed all his energy and learning to this end. Of course, few people enjoy his advantages; but we can all make a fresh effort to understand his un-shakeable moral principles and the history of human culture.

'To convey knowledge to the people, because this is the unique remedy for their problems ...' is how Tolstoy began his last work, *The Real Remedy,* written at Optin Pustin after his departure from Yasnaya Polyana.

As we come to the end of this century, famous for its unprecedented achievements in scientific and technical development, and move on to the beginning of the next, unheard of crimes have taken place, and people have shown terrible cruelty to each other and to nature. We have not been protected by our achievements; and there has been a growing comprehension of the importance and realism of Tolstoy's idealogy of culture before force, of the individual before the state, of common before private rights to land, of morality before lax commercial ethics. Morality was the central pivot of Tolstoy's philosophy. We cannot neglect his views in our search for an alternative form of society.

Tolstoy accumulated in his works the morality of the whole world. At the same time he portrayed the best features of the Russian character: humanitarianism, of which Dostoevsky also wrote, the passionate search for truth, that is, honesty and justice, democracy, creativity, moderation, presented in a unified and comprehensive form. Tolstoyan communities existed for some time after his death, and some are now reappearing. Once again, in such a genius as Tolstoy was, the Russian people can meet up with the cultures of the world; but the world must also understand Russia, which F. Tiutchev called 'the ununderstandable'.

The Moscow Leo Tolstoy Society continues the progressive activity that he started. This kind of activity goes along the following lines:
- setting up people's schools for everyday study;
- publishing religious books;
- setting up charitable organisations and committees;
- financing and organising communities of all kinds.

Because Tolstoy considered the moral perfection of humanity to be based on the labour of a free peasantry, he was interested in how to make their work on the land productive and how best to benefit both to the individual worker and to society. In this respect, he turned his attention to Henry George's proposal for single tax on the value of land. Tolstoy saw in this idea the possibility of a just regulation of land matters and the improvement of social relations as a whole, and he promoted Henry George's ideas in many different ways.

If Leo Tolstoy were alive in the year 1992, his support of Henry George's single tax on the value of land as a means of achieving common rights to it would, to my mind, certainly remain absolutely unchange-able. As President of the Leo Tolstoy Society, I share this opinion.

Tolstoy also turned to Henry George in his last moral-philosphical works, written shortly before his death. Both the idea itself of a single tax and Tolstoy's thoughts on these issues deserve the closest attention today, not least in Russia, which is currently undergoing painful economic and agricultural reform.

Tolstoy was a vegetarian and he considered the refusal to eat meat as the first step towards moral perfection, anticipating in this respect today's broad environmental movement, he was one of the first to recognise that the killing of animals, and pollution, would lead to ecological crisis, and his courageous championing of an unpolluted environment provides a shining example for contemporary "greens".

I hope that this book will contribute to a better knowledge of Tolstoy's philosophy and of Russian society, and, best of all, draw people together in new ideals of creativity, love and understanding.

Anatoly Gorelov.

Anatoly Al. Gorelov is a Doctor of Philosophy at the Academy of Sciences, Moscow. His publications include: *Ecology – Science – Simulation, Man – Harmony – Nature and The Split Man and The Integrity Of The Personality.*

His subjects are: Ecology, Psychology, Sociology, Anthropology, Religion, Art, Philosophy, Methodology of Science, Ethics and Aesthetics, Political Science and Old Russian Culture.

He is President of the Moscow Tolstoy Society.

Chapter 1
The final message

A prophet is not without honour, except in his own country, and among his own kin, and in his own house.
Jesus Christ (Mark 6, iv)

WHEN an eighty-two year old man, such as Count Leo Tolstoy was in October 1910, runs away from the home where he was born and has lived most of his life, deserting in the process the wife to whom he has been married for forty-eight years, one would rightly presume some fundamental and irremediable cleavage of ideas that makes any other course of action inconceivable. The average man of eighty-two, having few and relatively insignificant ideas, might indeed decide that it was too late to start a new life, and accordingly resolve to stay where he was and endure the short remainder of his present one. But then, Count Leo Tolstoy was not an average man.

Most people know that he was the author of *War and Peace* and *Anna Karenina,* two of the world's greatest novels; but this is about all they do know. Few realise, for example, that he also put his genius for social observation, which, together with his literary artistry, made him a great story-teller, to a more practical use. He was one of the few men in the nineteenth century who clearly saw the flaws in the social fabric that would lead to the catastrophes of the twentieth. Moreover, he had some definite proposals on what to do about them. It was to the exposition and attempted living-out of these proposals that he devoted the remaining thirty-three years of his life after completing *Anna Karenina.* Even his last full-length work of fiction, *Resurrection* (1899), was an obvious *roman à thèse,* and not only one thesis, but several related ones that perpetually occupied his mind.

1

In all this he was totally opposed by his arch-conservative wife; and, of their children, some took his part and some hers. This was his tragic dilemma. The strength of conviction that finally drove him, on the night of the 27th/28th October 1910, to make the final break may be assessed initially by the strength of the ties that bound him to his childhood home, Yasnaya Polyana, about one hundred miles south of Moscow, with all its cherished associations. The word 'home' is used advisedly; for, at one time during his wild youth, his gambling debts had led him to sell the old wooden building in which he had been born. So it had been bought, dismantled, carted away, and re-erected on the estate of a certain Gorokhov, where it went into terminal decay.

A home, however, consists of contents as well as of a shell. Its centre was and still is an eight-legged oak couch, probably made on the spot by household serf carpenters. It has three drawers, no back, but curved upholstered sides, fitted with sliding book-rests. Originally it was covered with green Russian leather; but this was later replaced with black oilcloth. It was the centre of the home, because on it had been born, not only Tolstoy himself, on the 28th August 1828, but also his brothers and most of his own children. The drawers were full of those manuscripts that he wished to keep secret from his beloved but inquisitive family.

The couch was the piece of furniture of which Tolstoy was most fond; but, in the room that he left more than eighty years ago, which is part of a new wing, his small writing desk is still to be seen. Here he kept, not, as one might expect, the materials of the writer's craft, but a set of tools, testifying to his devotion to manual labour. Tacked to the wall of the same room are some photographs and a print of the Sistine Madonna. Across this print for some reason are nailed rough bookshelves, on which stand the volumes of the *Brockhaus and Efron Encyclopaedia,* still in pristine condition; for Tolstoy was careful with his books, and, when he made marginal notes, made them lightly in pencil. In addition to these items, there are more tables, an ordinary paraffin lamp and three armchairs of dark and light oak. Under the lining of one of these he kept letters to his wife,

Sofya Andreyevna, née Behrs, to whom he had been married in 1862, to be handed to her after his death, and the manuscript of *Devil,* which he did not want her to see.

The contents of the rest of the house are similarly miscellaneous, consisting of odd pieces of furniture, old mirrors, two grand pianos, amateurish paintings by local serfs alongside a professional one of Tolstoy, bedsteads with brass knobs, and many small photographs and drawings. It is the usual array of ill-assorted articles among which people lived in the late Victorian era. Tolstoy's personal needs were far fewer than one would imagine to be appropriate to a man of his social status; but then, social status had long since ceased to interest him very much. Even bed linen was not particularly plentiful; and what there was had come there as part of Sofya's not very expensive trousseau. Before her time, Tolstoy had slept under a simple quilt with no sheets; and even before that, when there was a family gathering at Yasnaya Polyana, he and his brothers had slept on straw.

The house is situated in a park of two hundred and seventy acres, all that remains of the groves and plantations as they were in the days before Tolstoy sold off much of the estate to pay the expenses of his profligate youth. As much as a hundred and sixty-seven acres of this park are occupied by the apple orchard, which is one of the largest in Europe. The surrounding forests were once adapted, by the old rural craft of hedging on a large scale, to form an *abatis* or defensive system to protect the local inhabitants against raids by the Mongols at a time when they still ruled the Crimea. Through all this runs the main highway south, once a thoroughfare for armies, imperial retinues, stage coaches and pilgrims. Altogether, the house and park must have contained hundreds of memories for the aged writer. The strong force of attraction that bound him to them would not have been overcome save by an even stronger force of repulsion. This had taken a long time to build up.

From 1850 onwards, some early stirrings of social conscience had been overlaid by the creative impulse to transform his personal experiences into works of semi-fiction or fiction, so giving his readers a more than usually vivid impression of reliving them in their own imagination. In this way, he enjoyed for many years a literary gift possessed by only a few, first on his own, then with the co-operation as amanuensis of a loving wife, and reached a peak of fictional achievement in his two great masterpieces. He then sickened of it, and entered a mental wilderness from which at times it seemed to him that suicide offered the only means of escape.

He had some reason for not being pleased with himself. At the impressionable age of six, he had listened to his brother Nicholas telling him and the other boys, Sergey and Dmitri, that he knew a secret, and that, when the secret was revealed, all ills would disappear from the earth, and universal love prevail. The secret, said Nicholas, was carved on a green stick, which was buried on the edge of a ravine in the Zakaz Forest. The symbol of the quest for the green stick stayed at the back of Tolstoy's mind through a youth of broken resolutions and dissoluteness, an army life of decreasing commitment, and a literary career that in the end seemed to him mere self-indulgence.

What, he thought in 1879, two years after completing *Anna Karenina,* could be the possible justification for his idle and aimless life, supported by the labour of the wretchedly poor peasants on his estates, and protected by the forces of the State? For the next thirty years, he thought and wrote most of all about Christian ethics, the nature of the State, and the iniquity of private property in land. He also saw clearly that here were not three separate subjects, but a consistent political philosophy, in that the State acted mainly in defence of the landed interest, and was in turn supported by a Church founded on a false concept of Christ's significance for humanity. On the whole, he sought for solutions in the inner life of the individual; but, for a solution to the land question and concomitant social problems, he embraced a practical philosophy that was to achieve worldwide favour by the turn of the century. He gained thereby a popular following, but the enmity of the authorities and of half his family.

The enmity to make itself most felt was that of his wife, who had devoted endless time and trouble to copying and re-copying his earlier and politically neutral work. The fact was that, while the major part of his time and attention was devoted to the ills of the world and how they could be remedied in the future, hers was occupied with the problems of everyday life as it had to be lived there and then. She had planned the internal arrangements of the house, and devised the layout of the park. She supervised the domestic staff. She, above all, was the one to worry about financial provision for herself and the children, when this conflicted with her husband's ideals. She hated Tolstoy's ardent advocacy of a scheme for replacing taxation with ground rent as the source of public revenue, which would, if applied in Russia, have deprived the family of their traditional source of income. More personally, she hated Tolstoy's friend and literary agent V.G. Chertkov, whom she rightly suspected of influencing him to deprive her of the royalties from his pre-1881 novels and stories.

If Tolstoy had not suffered from an oversensitive conscience, it is possible that he and Sofya could have decided on a compromise; for, though his distaste for living off the unearned increment of land was perfectly reasonable, he need not have troubled himself about allowing her to continue to accept the royalties. A little more thought should have convinced him that labour is not exclusively manual, but that its wages are due also to non-manual workers, including those whose works of literary art contribute to the mental well-being of their fellow-creatures. As things were, however, the matter of the royalties was a cause of constant acrimonious quarrelling between them.

Nor did she ever allow him to forget about it. Whenever he retired for the night, he would hear her roaming round the house, searching among his papers for evidence of the conspiracy against her. It was the end. All he wanted was an opportunity to escape unobserved. It came at 5 a.m. on the 28th October, when there was an unusually prolonged silence. Only an hour before, Sofya had come into his room with a lighted candle, held it over his face, and asked him how he was; but now all was still. Rising quietly from his bed, he tiptoed to her door and listened. Not a sound. At last she was asleep.

Rapidly he dressed, went to waken his resident doctor friend Makovitsky and told him to pack any necessary medicines and come away with him. Then, while a maid packed some clothing for him, he woke his daughter Alexandra, told her he was leaving, and committed a few manuscripts to her care. His diaries he was going to take with him. An hour later, accompanied by the doctor, he left the house, like a desperate eighty-two year old King Lear, and made his way to the stables to order the coach to be prepared. Having said goodbye to Alexandra and another daughter, Varvara Feokritov, he drove to Shchyokino station to catch a train for Kazëlsk, twelve miles from the Shamordin Convent, to visit his sister Marya.

On the morning of the 31st, he set off with the doctor to catch the early train for Rostov-on-Don, having in the meantime caught a bad cold. In the circumstances, one might have expected him either to remain silent or to join in the usual conversational trivialities. But he knew that his time was short, and that inessentials must be laid aside in favour of matters of supreme importance. So, doubtless to the surprise of the young peasant who was sitting beside him, he began to lecture him, and before long all the occupants of the compartment, on the subject of the proposal of the American economist Henry George to achieve economic and social justice by replacing taxes on industry and trade with a single tax on the value of land.

Thus would be put into effect the twin principles that the fruits of a man's labour belong to himself alone, and that we all have an equal right of access to the resources of the Earth. Such a measure would also eliminate the power of one man to exploit another, either directly or by means of the machinery of State.

This was to be Tolstoy's last message for mankind; for his time was shorter that he knew. He never reached Rostov, but was so ill by the time the train drew in at Astapovo that he was taken off and put to bed in the stationmaster's house. On the 9th November 1910, he died there of pneumonia.

Chapter 2
The visionary freethinker

It is well to open one's mind, but only as a preliminary to
closing it ... for the supreme act of judgment and selection.
Irving Babbitt

P IONEERS of social change have never had an easy time of
it, as Molière, another great literary artist, was well aware.
Alceste, the main character of his *Le Misanthrope* (1666), is
shown reacting in vain against the frivolities and insincerities of
the idle rich in the Paris of Louis XIV and against the
corruption of the contemporary legal system. Even his friend
Philinte can find nothing more helpful to say to him than:

Et c'est une folie à nulle autre seconde
De vouloir se mêler de corriger le monde.[1]

And it is a folly second to none
To want to become involved in putting the world right.

Philinte thought that his friend, though correct in principle,
was wasting his time trying to put right what were, after all,
minor abuses. It would have surpassed the genius, even of a
Molière, to have restrained within the limits of comedy the
likely reactions to Alceste had he, like Jacques Turgot, Finance
Minister of a hundred years later, or Henry George and Leo
Tolstoy two hundred years later, proposed what amounted to a
social revolution. Let us have a closer look at this human inertia
and resistance to change.

The genetic inheritance of each individual human being is
settled at the moment of conception, and is the sole
determinant, barring accident, of his physical, instinctual,

7

intellectual and moral standing up to the moment of birth. From then on, society takes over, and begins to expose him to a variety of generally accepted practices, including those related to language, costume, habitation, deportment, schooling, religion – everything, in fact, that is a distinctive mark of human relationships at the particular time and place. The infant accepts most of this without question; but the time surely comes when he will question some of it, and test his own will-power against that of his parents, his teachers at school, his first employer, a policeman or anybody who comes along. The typical youngster may gain his way in one or two matters, and conform in the rest; but it is more likely that he will end by conforming in everything.

Beyond the immediate surroundings of each individual, there are the wider entities of the nation, the continent and the world. Few people will submit the customs of these to examination, especially such as are in line with the common inclinations towards reverence and awe, combativeness and recognition of territory and social hierarchy. Take a man into the incense-laden atmosphere of a church, and he will bow down and worship. Show him a uniform that he is to wear while fighting other people designated as enemies, and he will put it on. Take him to a coronation, or a state opening of parliament, and he will become a respecter of the 'powers that be'. Show him a notice saying 'Trespassers will be prosecuted', and he will back respectfully away.

This is not to say that there will be no dissidents; but that they will substitute in some cases their natural inclination for the behaviour that is expected of them. They will stay away from church; leave the battlefield, throw away their uniform and return home; break the law or a few fences, and either thrive by doing so or go to prison. What they will not do on the whole is sit down, imagine an alternative society and commit a plan of it to writing.

Such a course of action must have been particularly difficult in the civilisation of Europe and western Asia in the first decade of the twentieth century. It had existed for a thousand years, was supported by the combined influences of the school, the sword and the altar, and was deeply ingrained in the consciousness of the vast majority of people. True it had had its setbacks of revolutions and wars, and offered far more in of material rewards to some than to others; but such things appeared to be part of the stuff of natural existence, and to question them appeared, and indeed to many still appears, akin to madness.

It is all the more remarkable, therefore, when there arises such a man as Count Leo Tolstoy, who looks with fresh eyes at every aspect of the world about him, as if he had just been born in the full possession of all his mature faculties, or as if he were a visitor from another planet, standing amazed before new scenes, unfamiliar thought processes, and strange ways of behaving. To compound the unlikelihood of the mere existence of this man, he had the capacity to embody his thoughts in a lively and virile prose that makes the reader gasp, both at the boldness of his pronouncements and at the modesty with which he himself regarded his abilities. Here, for example, is his friend and translator Aylmer Maude writing about a conversation held with him in about the year 1900:

'I divide men', said Tolstoy, 'into two lots. They are freethinkers, or they are not freethinkers. I am not speaking of the Freethinkers who form a political party in Germany, nor of the agnostic English Freethinkers, but I am using the word in its simplest meaning'.[2]

Maude explains that the kind of freethinker Tolstoy had in mind was the man who is not afraid to follow a line of reasoning to its logical end, careless of whether it clashes with existing social customs or interferes with his personal privileges or preconceived beliefs.

This definition, one would think, does at the very least apply to all those ranking as scientists, *people who know*. Even while all around them are manipulating or ignoring facts to suit their own purposes, surely the scientists will hold fast to the truth and nothing but the truth? Unfortunately, the answer is no, not always.

A particularly sensitive line of scientific enquiry is the one that concerns our human origins. It must by now be a very small minority that goes for its information about these to chapters 2 and 3 of the *Book of Genesis;* but very many more, even if they accept in principle the theory of Charles Darwin, shocking in his time, that the human race is a product of slow development from a type ancestral to ourselves and to other present-day primates, like to think that we are the culmination of a direct line of peaceful vegetarian animals, such as the chimpanzee on the whole is now. Perhaps we may have lapsed a little after attaining our present biological status, and taken to meat-eating and mortal quarrels on an ever-increasing scale; but all this is by the way. Our natural bent is to be harmless and virtuous. As Jean-Jacques Rousseau (1712-1778), the philosopher who above all others supplied the theoretical basis of the French Revolution, so succinctly put it:

Que la nature a fait l'homme heureux et bon, mais que la société le déprave et le rend misérable.[3]

Nature made man happy and good, but how society depraves him and makes him wretched!

This is what many people like to think; and this is what Tolstoy, a life-long admirer of Rousseau, liked to think too; but, in his time, there was no more reliable information available. Had he still been alive in 1957, when it did become available, he would certainly have approved of its author, the free-thinking and iconoclastic Raymond A. Dart, Head of the Department of Anatomy at the University of the Witwatersrand in the Transvaal; and he would have made allowances in his theory of society, which nobody else has yet done to the satisfaction of either the academic world or the world at large, for an alternative estimate of human nature.

Dart[4] considered he had proved that creatures now generally accepted as human ancestors, namely members of the species *Australopithecus Africanus* (or *Prometheus*), had, between two and three million years ago, used certain antelope bones, not only as weapons of the chase and butchery tools, but also as a means of settling differences among themselves. The evidence was that, at Makapansgat in the Transvaal, non-hominid fossil bones found in conjunction with those of the hominid included antelope bones of the types in question in much larger numbers than would justify any theory of random distribution. In other words, they were the result of intelligent and purposeful selection, not the remains of four-legged carnivores' meals.

Furthermore, numerous baboon skulls from the same period, found at this and other neighbouring sites, showed clear signs of fracture as a result of blows struck with the humeri (or upper foreleg bones) of antelopes. There was also a similarly damaged *Australopithecine* jawbone, indicating that murder with a blunt instrument was a possibility even at this remote time. This in itself may mean nothing, but, taken in conjunction with evidence[5] of organised fighting among Neanderthalers in northern Yugoslavia, the testimony of early history, and intertribal warfare among modern primitive peoples, it could be highly significant. If there is a salient inbred tendency in man to be an armed killer, then any plan for a future society based on the unqualified assumption that he is naturally harmless and inoffensive is unrealistic. This is not to say that he does not also have diametrically opposed tendencies, which prevail with suitable encouragement. Unfortunately, it is too often the killer instinct that is encouraged.

Dart's thesis therefore deserved very serious consideration, but failed to receive it. Instead, the scientists to whom it was presented ignored his statistical analysis of the fossil bones, and dismissed the collection as the work of hyaenas, which it most evidently is not. In a precisely similar fashion, the philosophical works of Tolstoy deserved at the time, and still deserve now, the consideration of all who genuinely wish to help to bring about a better world. Instead, our deeply conservative society has chosen, on the whole, to misunderstand, misrepresent, or simply to ignore them. Apart from those bearing mainly on religion, which pose a negligible threat at present to those who benefit from social injustice, they have been alllowed to go out of print in England.

But Tolstoy's denunciation of the injustice of land monopoly carried further implications. As the owner of large estates himself, he was working to undermine his personal position of privilege, and exposing himself to the accusation of being a traitor to his class. By preaching Henry George's remedy, he made it certain that the seal of official disapproval would be put on his economic thought.

As if all this were not enough, he identified the unfair distribution of land as the root cause of gross differences in the power associated with wealth, which could be maintained only by Nation/States based on violence. Such violence, applied by armed forces to subdue domestic unrest, to conquer foreign lands, and to secure foreign markets for goods unsaleable at home by reason of poverty, he demonstrated to be contrary to true Christian principles. Luckily for the Nation/States, they were, as he saw it, supported by perverted churches, who ignored the teachings of Jesus Christ in favour not only of dogma concerning his origin and destiny, but also of ritual designed to 'hypnotise' (his own word) the mass of the population.

In what follows, we shall attempt to conform to Tolstoy's method of freethinking by submitting his doctrines to analysis, and comparing them with the criticisms they have attracted. Were they valid at the time? What is their relevance to the problems of the present day? Tolstoy regarded his ideas as a rounded whole; and so do we. As a matter of convenience, however, we shall consider them separately, beginning with his conception of Christianity, which influences and controls all the rest.

Chapter 3
The doctrinal dispute

To be like Christ is to be a Christian.
William Penn.

THE overall impression one gains from a reading of Tolstoy's philosophical works is that for a final solution to social problems he relied mainly on individual moral change. This is the biblical *metanoia,* generally translated as 'repentance', as good an example as any of the limitations of a word-for-word translation of the gospels, and the need for either a knowledge of Greek or the services of a reliable commentator, or both, if one is to gain an adequate understanding of their message. What should be understood by *metanoia* is either a 'change of mind' or a 'change in the inner man'. Tolstoy himself took the trouble, unusually late in life, to learn Greek, solely to make sure that he had extracted from the gospels everything that could help him, not only with compensating for his dissolute youth, but also with his self-imposed task of contributing to the establishment of the Kingdom of God on Earth in place of the society based historically on the spoliation and violence that he saw about him.

To concentrate his mind to the uttermost, he produced his own translation of the gospels, which differed rather markedly from its predecessors. By these means, he satisfied himself that the core of the Christian message is in *Matthew v, 21-48,* a part of the collection of sayings that we cite collectively as the 'Sermon on the Mount'.[1] Thereafter he was to refer to this passage as the 'Five commandments of Christ'. They are as follows:

1. The Mosaic Law laid down that 'whoever kills shall be liable

to judgment'. Christ extended the prohibition against killing to include what generally leads up to it in individual cases, namely anger. The best texts leave it at that; but others add the two words 'without cause'.

Confronted with this, Tolstoy drew the rational conclusion that the added words destroyed the whole meaning of the rest. He was horrified to discover, on consulting the interpretations of the Fathers of the Church, that their attention was chiefly directed towards explaining when anger is, or is not, excusable. This was to be a significant element in his total disillusionment with the orthodox presentation of Christianity.

2. The Mosaic Law prohibited adultery; but Christ prohibited the very thought of it. He also set his face against the easy process of marriage dissolution *(Deuteronomy xxiv, 1)*, whereby a husband may give his wife a certificate of divorce because 'he has found some indecency in her'. Christ went further, and laid it down that divorce is inadmissible 'except on the ground of unchastity'.

Here Tolstoy's taste for unqualified definition, generally so admirable, led him astray. *Parektos logou porneias* really does mean 'except on the ground of unchastity', and applies to the wife. Tolstoy thought it meant 'besides the sin of dissoluteness', and applied to the husband. At the time he put these ideas together (1884), he was fully convinced of the need for marriage and its maintenance intact; but later (1889), when he had quarrelled with his wife over his wish to renounce his property, he turned to the opinion that marriage is an obstacle in the way of a truly Christian life. On this occasion, it is to be feared, his private feelings overcame his philosophical detachment.

3. When it comes to Christ's amendment of the old law concerning oaths, Tolstoy makes a vital observation. Here is the text from *Matthew v, 33-37:*

> Again you have heard that it was said to the men of old, 'You shall not swear falsely, but shall perform to the Lord what you have sworn'. But I say to you, Do not swear at all, ... Let what you say

be simply 'Yes' or 'No'; anything more than this comes of evil.

At first sight, this appeared to Tolstoy to be a self-evident proposition, putting in a general form particular ancient injunctions not to swear by God, by heaven, by the earth, by Jerusalem or by one's own head. Those well-known non-swearers, the Quakers, are more specific, and point out that taking an oath is a confession of a double standard of truth. If I merely say that I will do something or that such and such is so, you believe me at your own risk; but, if I say it on oath, then you may trust me. This evidently is not good enough: satisfactory human relationships require openness and truthfulness.

On second thoughts, after he had consulted the commentators, to whom he ironically acknowledges an obligation, Tolstoy saw more significance in this passage; for they were careful to explain that Christ's words should not be taken to apply to a citizen's oath of loyalty to those in authority. When one considers Christ's habitual attitude of disrespect towards the authorities of his own time, one can see some sense in Tolstoy's opinion that this is an instance of the sinister contemporary alliance between Church and State.

4. The precept of Christ *(Matthew v, 38-41)* annulling the old law of retaliation was, says Tolstoy, the first that he understood, and the one that helped him to understand all the rest. It is therefore worth quoting in full:

> Do not resist one who is evil. But if any one strikes you on the right cheek, turn to him the other also; and if any one would sue you and take your coat, let him have your cloak as well; and if any one forces you to go one mile, go with him two miles.

This precept was to occupy a central position in Tolstoy's thought on a variety of subjects, including the unlikely one of economic reform. Whenever he mentioned violence, he would have been thinking of this text, which was closely associated in his mind with the last of Christ's 'five commandments':

5. You have heard that it was said, 'You shall love your neighbour and hate your enemy'. But I say to you, Love your enemies and pray for those who persecute you, ...

As Tolstoy justly observed, a 'neighbour' in Jewish thought meant a fellow-Jew, and an 'enemy' a member of a hostile foreign nation. The concept was to be put into practice in the furious rebellion against Roman rule that culminated in the mass suicide at Masada in A.D.73. Tolstoy's recognition of the meaning of the contrasting terms made it easier for him, and for us, to see how it is possible to love an enemy; for, after all, to expect someone to love a personal enemy is asking rather too much. Christ himself befriended a Roman centurion; and the parable of the good Samaritan showed how, in certain circumstances, an 'enemy' might come to be a 'neighbour'.

Such was the main thrust of Tolstoy's religious thought. What he rejected may be ascertained in detail from his own version of the gospels, in which anything savouring of the supernatural, from the virgin birth to the ascension, will not be found. He did, however, believe that human life has its origin in an infinite divine source. It was only to be expected that his radical re-interpretation of Christianity would excite comment, from friendly criticism to outright condemnation; and that in fact is what happened.

Aylmer Maude sums up his religious doctrines with evident approval, pointing out that any attempt to define God as a person or persons responsible for the creation of the material universe saddles us with the admission that God created evil as well as good – a difficulty that nobody has as yet managed convincingly to get round. If, on the contrary, we confine ourselves to personal experience, 'we may be as sure as Socrates was that we are in touch with the Eternal Goodness. We know not how to speak of this power within us and outside us, except to say that it is Love: God is Love'.[2]

In another essay,[3] Maude writes about Tolstoy's high opinion of Matthew Arnold's works on religion.[4] The general verdict was to put his poetical works first, his critical works second, and his religious works third; but Tolstoy would reverse this order. It need not therefore surprise us to see Maude referring to 'personal experience' and a 'power within us and outside us'; for these are palpable reflections of Arnold's thought.

Arnold himself, in an essay on Tolstoy,[5] found much that was 'questionable' among much that was 'ingenious and powerful' in Tolstoy's Biblical exegesis. This too is hardly surprising: we have noticed something questionable ourselves. It cannot, however, have been too serious; for the only point that he wished to make at the time of writing (1887) was that Christianity depends as much on the 'sweetness and reasonableness' of its founder as on 'any series of maxims' that his followers recorded. Despite all else, there is no mistaking the general air of friendly agreement with Tolstoy's doctrines. The two men had met in London in 1861; so it could have been the case with both Arnold and Maude that Tolstoy's vehemence of speech and obvious guilelessness helped to strengthen the impression made on them by his writings.

One of his most modern critics, A.N. Wilson, born too late to have any such advantage, was initially too much at the mercy of his own conventional upbringing to have any sympathy with Tolstoy's freethinking in the matter of religion. In a forty-two page chapter entitled 'The holy man', there appears this significant passage:

> ... From beginning to end, the New Testament is caught up in mystery. Its difficulties will never be solved by scholars, though there is no harm in their trying. Glints of what the mystery was, and is, are only discernible through worship.
> Tolstoy had tried that, but it did not answer. His rationalistic, nineteenth-century knees lacked health until they had stopped genuflecting. But he was enough, *au fond,* a Russian Orthodox to know that he could not refuse to worship without, as it were, divine sanction. And so the Gospels themselves had to be looted and plundered and robbed of the mystery which is their essence.[6]

These are views that Wilson, by his own later admission,[7] would no longer expound. Here is another modern critic, E.B.

Greenwood, but one who is unequivocally on Tolstoy's side:

> He does not use the wretched Pascalian argument that we should take holy water and stupefy ourselves if we want to find faith. On the contrary, his whole effort in his religious works is to make a bold attempt to separate the essential truths of the faith he sees around him from the ignorance and superstition in which they are embedded.[8]

Greenwood has used the word 'stupefy', Maude's translation of one of Tolstoy's favourites, to render the French word 'abêtir'. Pascal wrote as follows:

> Suivez la manière par où ils ont commencé: c'est en faisant tout comme s'ils croyaient, en prenant de l'eau bénite, en faisant dire des messes, etc. ... Naturellement même cela vous fera croire et vous abêtira.[9]

> *Follow the way by which they [i.e. other unbelievers] began: that is, in doing everything as if they believed, taking holy water, having masses said, etc. ... It is only natural that that will make you believe, and will stupefy you.*

It is our impression that many modern church-goers would side with the old Wilson, and claim that the Bible must be accepted or rejected in its entirety. But have they no conception of the period of time, to be counted in thousands of years, and the measureless human labour, that went into its composition? Are we to assume that, without exception, the authors waited for divine inspiration before they performed the equivalent for their time of setting pen to paper? Perhaps such concepts, divorced from common experience, go most of the way towards accounting for the empty pews on Sundays.

All this is a great pity; for, even given a population that was 100 per cent rationalist, the teachings of Christ and the example of his sweet reasonableness could still be of inestimable value. Let us consider an extreme hypothesis, going well beyond Tolstoy's in its rationalism, and supported by the available evidence. Living matter arose through the action of inter-stellar radiation on primordial slime, and, throughout billions of years, has been progressively modified by the action of this same radiation on the genes of individuals. Inefficient species so evolved have been removed by death. The human story began twenty million years ago when the unspecialised ape *Proconsul* entered the arid African Pliocene Age as a tree-dwelling vegetarian, to emerge after about seventeen or eighteen million non-fossil-bearing years as Raymond Dart's upright-walking carnivorous ape *Australopithecus,* capable of violence against his own kind, and a habitual user of weapons.

In these circumstances, would it not be helpful to regard Christ as a human being endowed with a mutant gene that not only removed his own capacity for hate and violence, but also made him subconsciously aware that these qualities no longer favoured the survival of the human species, but on the contrary tended towards its destruction?

This is a message that is needed more than ever now that the antelope humerus of *Australopithecus* has been succeeded by nuclear missiles, poison gas and deadly viruses. The established Churches still do not feature prominently in opposition to war, even by such means; and indeed the aircraft, named Enola Gay, that dropped the first atomic bomb on Hiroshima was blessed by a U.S. Army chaplain before its departure. In Tolstoy's time the danger had long been apparent; and he inveighed mercilessly against the Russian Orthodox Church for its support of a State based on, and maintained by, violence, and for its specious arguments in favour of neglecting Christian principles on this account. For example, he quotes the argument that the injunction not to resist evil by violence applies only to an individual suffering under it personally. When others are so suffering, it is his duty to do so. He then goes on:

> If one's personal judgement is to decide the question of what con-
> stitutes danger for other people, there is no case of violence that
> cannot be justified on the ground of danger threatening some-
> body.[10]

It need not be supposed that the Russian Orthodox Church is the only one that can be accused of serving the interests of the State by revising the Christian religion. A simple test is to read the Apostles' Creed and to note how it jumps from *'born of the Virgin Mary'* to *'suffered under Pontius Pilate'*, as if nothing worth mentioning had occurred in between. Another is to consider the following passage from the English *Catechism:*

> My duty towards my Neighbour is to love him as myself, and to do to all men as I would they should do unto me: To love, honour and succour my father and mother: To honour and obey the King, and all that are put in authority under him: To submit myself to all my governors, teachers, spiritual pastors and masters: To order myself lowly and reverently to all my betters: ... .

The first two injunctions are in the pure spirit of Christianity. The third emphasises family loyalty, the natural source of continuous security from generation to generation. Christ certainly demanded of his immediate companions that they should leave their families and follow him; but this was to meet the exigencies of the first mission, and can hardly be taken as a message for all time. The rest, from 'To honour and obey the King' onwards, is wholly foreign to the spirit of the gospels, and directly contrary to the example set us by Christ in his own life. It can have been composed only with the cynical intention of bending Christian morality to suit the temporal and materialistic requirements of an unscrupulous ruling class, the nature of which will be made more and more plain in due course.

It could also be significant that, whereas the injunction of *Exodus, xx, 13* is 'Thou shalt not kill', that of the English *Catechism* is 'Thou shalt do no murder'. Some difference must be intended; and the most likely one is that between killing for a personal reason, which is murder and therefore wrong, and killing by the orders of those 'set in authority' under the King, which by the new dispensation becomes permissible. Tolstoy recognised no such difference, and neither, we can be sure, would Christ have done.

There is nothing surprising about any of this when one

considers the circumstances in which the first vernacular catechisms were introduced. Unrest among the peasantry of Europe had been of common occurrence at the time of the Reformation; and, in particular, the Peasants' Revolt in Germany (1524-6) had given the rich and powerful a very nasty shock. It was in response to these events that Martin Luther, who sympathised with the peasants' cause, but not with their methods, produced his two catechisms in 1529. 'Let the people be taught', he said, 'let schools be opened for the poor, let the truth reach them in simple words in their own mother tongue, and they will believe'.

In England, the *Book of Common Prayer,* containing the *Catechism,* fell into disuse during the Civil War, 'the late unhappy confusions' as it is described in the preface, but came out in a new edition 'upon His Majesty's happy Restoration', or, to be quite accurate, two years later in 1662. It was well timed: the ruling classes were soon to be in need of all the ignorant docile men they could muster to fight the Dutch for them, and to lay the foundations of the British Empire in the east.

In Russia, the Orthodox Church re-affirmed its union with the autocratic monarchy at the outbreak of the first world war. The Tsar's manifestos declaring war on Germany and Austria were read out in churches before being posted up outside. They were also read out in the Nikolai Hall of the Winter Palace, Petersburg; and prayers were said before an icon of Our Lady of Kazan. When the Tsar and Tsarina went out on to the balcony overlooking Palace Square, they saw before them a great concourse of royal portraits, national flags and religious banners. The insignia of the Christian religion would not be considered necessary by the new régime, already biding its time.

Chapter 4
The critical foul

Now the melancholy god protect thee, and the tailor make
thy doublet of changeable taffeta, for thy mind is a very
opal.
William Shakespeare.

TOLSTOY'S ideas on the reform of human society challenged so many assumptions, old and crusted, but logically indefensible, that attacks on him of various kinds became inevitable. One of these methods of attack, which should be regarded with contempt, was the literary equivalent of the deliberate foul in association football. The common description of this as 'playing the man instead of the ball' makes the analogy clearer. We have already come across examples in A.N. Wilson's chapter headed sarcastically 'The Holy man', with his implication that Tolstoy was weak-kneed, and his use of the emotive words 'looted', 'plundered' and 'robbed' to describe the omission of miraculous elements from Tolstoy's version of the gospels (Ch.3). In football the practice spoils the spectators' pleasure in a skilful game, gives a momentary unfair advantage, and, carried to extremes, turns a fine contest into a coarse brawl. The corresponding critical offence is to despair of refuting an author's ideas, and to call them into question by casting aspersions on the author personally. It can have the far more serious result of ensuring the general rejection of ideas that would have been capable otherwise of furthering human progress, or removing barriers to it.

Variations of this form of attack were to say that he was erratic and inconsistent, said one thing and did another, said one thing one day and another the next, and was generally

22

speaking liable to change his mind.

These accusations are true, as they are for the majority of mankind. Tolstoy's habit of mixing with the peasantry, and wearing their traditional grey flannel smock while at home, never completely replaced his pride in belonging to an aristocratic family. Similarly, Slavdom formed an important part of his sense of personal identity, but did not prevent him from being open to western influences, those, for example, of Rousseau and of Matthew Arnold. Then again, the unease induced in him by his landed property did not always stand in his way when he heard of more going at a bargain price. Most striking of all, but least relevant to an appraisal of his writings, is the contrast between his professed asceticism and his known continuing sexual activity past the age of seventy.

The diversity of his inconsistency may have set him aside from ordinary men in yet one more way; but it was this very diversity, this capacity for seeing life from so many points of view, that made him the great novelist that he was. It must further be urged in justification that some of his alleged inconsistency was a process of development from one phase of life to another, which he did not afterwards reverse. From a hunter and meat-eater he became a vegetarian and respecter of all animal life; and his guilt about landownership in the end overcame him to the extent that he gave away his estates, though only to his family.

It was probably his marriage to Sofya Behrs in 1862, and the satisfactions of family life, that began to make him as much like anybody else as he was capable of being. To begin with, his very physical appearance set him apart, as his eldest daughter Tatyana makes clear:

> I remember him when he was still young. His beard was auburn, almost red; he had black, slightly wavy hair and pale blue eyes. Those eyes were sometimes gentle and caressing, sometimes merry, sometimes severe and inquisitorial. He was tall, broad-shouldered, well-muscled, yet very quick and dexterous in all his movements.
>
> At that time his hair had not yet turned white and his face was still

unmarked by the suffering and the scalding tears that furrowed his features later on, during that period when he was searching so fervently and in such loneliness for the meaning of life.
As he grew older so he went white, began to stoop, and shrank in size, while his pale eyes became gentler, and sometimes sad.
We rarely heard reproaches from his lips, either as children or when we grew up, but when papa said something you didn't forget it, and you did as he said without fail.[1]

The same eye-witness testifies to his children's love for him, his cleverness at inventing games and his general willingness to enter into their activities. All the same, before they knew what he was doing when he was shut up in his room alone, they sensed that it must have been both necessary and important. Even when Tatyana saw him do something that she felt to be horrible and disgusting, as when he took a wounded woodcock out of his game-bag and casually killed it with one of its own feathers, her shock was tempered by the feeling that if her father could do such a thing, perhaps it was not very bad. Later in life, of course, he would not have shot the woodcock in the first place.

Even more to the point is Tatyana's observation, remarkable for a child of nine years, of her father's relationships with other grownups. The family was spending the summer of 1873 on their estate on the steppes near Samara (the modern Kuibyshev); and Tolstoy would sometimes take them visiting. Here is what she has to say:

> Papa could always find things to talk about that would interest the various people he met. With the mullah he discussed religion, with Mikhail Ivanovich he joked, and with the peasants he talked about spring sowings, horses, the weather ... And they all responded with trust and simplicity.[2]

This is what is commonly known as empathy, the power of entering into another's personality, and imaginatively experiencing his experiences. It made him a great novelist – this much has been generally acknowledged. It also gave him the capacity for getting to the roots of the world's troubles, and seeing that half-measures, such as satisfy the conscience of the common run of humanity, would never bring about permanent results. General recognition of this quality has yet to come.

The overall impression Tatyana gives of him up to 1879, when the second of the great novels was finished, was one of a normal, but somewhat larger than life, father of a happy and united family. His later, unconventional activities and writings were indeed to divide it; but she shared his views and remained loyal to the end.

His life before his marriage had, in contrast, been erratic in the extreme, proliferating in plans for self-improvement, soon abandoned, broken resolutions to shun gambling or irregular sexual relations, and abortive attempts to choose a wife. The last of these attempts involved a certain Katerina Alexandrovna, about whom his sister Marya had written to him in September 1861:

> If it were to work out, wouldn't you soon be asking yourself, 'Why did I do it?' Wouldn't you, one fine morning, quietly begin to hate your wife, thinking, 'If only I hadn't married ... ?'[3]

When Tolstoy protested about this estimate of his likely behaviour, Marya, in a letter reminiscent of a piece of dialogue by Molière, changed her ground, and advised him to propose. As she must have guessed he would, he then withdrew. What she predicted happened in fact with Sofya Behrs, not once but many times.

Nor was this all: his temper was subject to frequent changes from one extreme to another. On some days he could be the life and soul of a party, singing and dancing and playing games. On others, which his daughter evidently preferred to forget, he could be a surly recluse or even worse. On one occasion, he found the pregnant Sofya sitting on the floor tidying the contents of a drawer, and terrified the household with his berserk rage at what he thought to be an unwise activity. How do we account for this unpredictable behaviour? In an age that has known two world wars, and many minor ones since, there must be few people who have had no experience of such cases – men, for example, who had been through the first, normally friendly and cheerful, but whom their wives were afraid to leave alone with their sons, in case they beat them savagely with a strap on some slight pretext. Then, when the second came with its air raids, they could be found crying underneath the table. Such can be the effects of prolonged exposure to shellfire; and Tolstoy spent two years under British and French shellfire in Sevastopol. They must have left their mark on him.

So far as I know, this explanation has not yet been advanced to account for his violent temper, so contrary to his Christian ethic of love. The main point to be made, however, is that none of this has the slightest relevance to his philosophy of life. It is useless to say: 'He blew hot and cold; he backed and filled; he flew off the handle for no reason at all; like the moon, he had an infinite number of phases; therefore his ideas are worthless'. They may or may not be; but at least they deserve to be considered separately on their merits.

Chapter 5
Violent birth of the State

I like the dreams of the future better than the history of the past.
Thomas Jefferson.

S OCIAL pressures to influence the individual's attitude to
the *status quo* are exerted with particular force for the
moulding of opinions on the Nation/State. Those of us, for
example, who went to school in England during the twenties
and thirties will remember that history lessons were devoted
largely to the growth of the British Empire, and that, at a later
stage perhaps, we had lessons on the British constitution
designed to prove to us how lucky we were to be allowed to
govern ourselves, in contrast to those who had to submit to the
will of a dictator.

Furthermore, there were facilities, carefully graded according
to the status of the school, for preparing boys for service as
officers or other ranks in the forces that would be needed during
the next war to protect our possessions and privileges against
envious enemies. These instructions were probably acceptable to
most; but there would still be the occasional rebel with his
doubts about the Empire, and suspicions that what was called
democracy was in reality a manifestation of what Stephen
Leacock, Canadian humorist and professor of economics,
termed 'genial humbug'. The powers of the electorate, and
even of Members of Parliament, were illusory, such a boy would
have felt, and the means of compulsion would be ready to be
used as a last resort.

As we shall see, Tolstoy was not misled by the 'genial
humbug' into thinking that the English or French States
differed in kind from that of the Russian, which was

unashamedly autocratic, and regularly used means of compulsion as a first resort. It is obvious from his copious footnotes
that he was well aware that this situation had not arisen
overnight, but was the result of a long historical process.
English-speaking readers, therefore, will be better equipped to
see nineteenth and early twentieth century Russia as it were
through Tolstoy's eyes, and to judge the validity both of his
political views, and of his critics' appraisal of them, if they
possess at the outset some outline knowledge of what he knew
in more detail.

The beginnings of Russian history melt into legend. Three
brothers from the land of Rus, possibly part of Sweden, are said
to have been invited over as rulers by turbulent tribes who lived
in the forests between Lake Ladoga and the upper reaches of the
Dnieper. It is not in fact unlikely that something of the sort did
happen; for we know that Scandinavia was a main area of
recruitment for the famous Varangian Guard of the Eastern
Emperors. What more likely than that some of the young
adventurers thus attracted should have dropped off on the river
route across Russia to form, as did many of their fellow-
countrymen in other parts of Europe, a dominant military caste
among a subject population?

What is certain is that, within two centuries, they and their
descendants had extended their dominion as far as Kiev, and
that they treated the country as if it were a vast family estate,
paying them rent and governed according to generally understood rules of inheritance. These rules may have been understood, but they were not always observed by princes with armed
followers, predisposed to solving their differences by means of
violence. As a result, by the beginning of the 13th century, the
principality of Muscovy was well on the way to becoming the
nucleus of the future Russian Empire.

In 1238, however, a new band of military adventurers arrived
on the scene, Tartars from the 'Golden Horde', as the west of
the Mongol Empire was known. They kept on the whole to their
pastoral way of life, but built themselves a capital, Sarai, on the
banks of the lower Volga, and exacted tribute over a wide area.
It is hardly to be imagined that the Russian princes had ever had

scruples about appropriating for themselves anything produced by the labouring population in excess of a bare livelihood; so the latter would in the long run have stood to lose no more on the advent of the new exploiters. On the contrary, the princes, under the requirement to pay tribute, would have become in effect their new masters' agents for collecting the rent. This new way of life demanded the acquisition of new habits. Instead of fighting among themselves, the princes intrigued against each other at the court of the local Khan in Sarai, or at the camp of the Grand Khan in Karakorum, Mongolia, where in any case they had to go to be confirmed in their functions. These lessons on the nature of autocratic rule would be of lasting effect.

With the weakening of the Tartar hegemony after about two centuries, the princes of Muscovy began once more to assert themselves, conspiring with Tartar generals, intercepting the tribute for their own use, and assuming the leadership of a patriotic movement. They were therefore well placed, after the final defeat of the Tartars, to resume their policy of aggression, to extend their territories at the expense of their weaker neighbours, and to proclaim themselves Caesars, or Tsars, of all Russia. This process of absorption was completed between 1462 and 1584 by the Tsars Ivan III, Basil and Ivan IV, commonly known as Ivan the Terrible.

Among the last of the independent states to disappear were Pskov and Great Novgorod, both of which had republican constitutions of long standing. In Novgorod alone, the massacre, over a period of time, of more than 60,000 people is said to have been required before all hope of the revival of its constitution was abandoned. Also of significance for the future was the recognition of the new Tsars by the Eastern Orthodox Church, and the coronation in 1547 of Ivan the Terrible by its Metropolitan. From this time on they regarded themselves as the Lord's Anointed, far above the next highest in the land, and surrounded themselves with barbaric splendour, including a guard of young nobles dressed in gorgeous costumes and armed with silver halberds. They indulged themselves in such luxury, it must be remembered, at the expense of a peasantry restrained by force.

The clearest possible evidence of this dates from the next reign, that of Theodore (1584-98), during which the real ruler was his brother-in-law, Boris Godunov. The comparatively small number of princes, nobles and others who had compelled acceptance of their title of ownership to this thinly-populated country were unable, so long as labourers were free to move in search of higher wages, to maintain at a maximum the rental incomes on which they relied for their idle and extravagant style of living. So they secured the enactment of laws for the binding of labourers to the soil *(adscriptio glebae)*. This was the beginning of Russian serfdom.

This reign also saw the beginning of a closer relationship between Church and State, comparable with the assumption by Henry VIII of the headship of the Church of England. Hitherto the highest authority in the Russian Church had been the Metropolitan, who was formally subject to the Patriarch of Constantinople. But Constantinople had fallen to the Turks in 1453; and, while the Tsars were claiming, by virtue of the marriage of Ivan III to the niece of the last Emperor, Constantine Palaeologus, to be his legitimate successors, it seemed altogether appropriate that the Russian Church should be governed by an independent Patriarch. For a while the relationship between the religious and secular authorities even became one of blood; for Michael Romanov, who came to the throne in 1613 on the strength of his mother's descent from the previous dynasty, was also the son of the Patriarch Philaret. These two ruled on an equal footing; but all except one of Philaret's successors, the Patriarch Nikon, abandoned any such pretension.

Roughly from the beginning of the seventeenth century onwards, or the end of the reign of the Tsar Theodore, new considerations enter into the study of international affairs. Before this time, on the whole, wars had been fought with the object of territorial gain and additional rental income. After this time, the emphasis shifts to wars for foreign markets. The reason, in western Europe particularly, was that, with the concentration of land-holding into fewer and fewer hands, land-holders became richer and those who were forced to sell their labour to others became poorer. Capital for the production and exchange of goods thus came to be drawn from rent rather than from wages; and a class of land-and-capital monopolists began to grow. A further and more dangerous effect of the increasing disparities in wealth was that, taken as a whole, the class of person whose labour brought the goods into being was too poor to buy them all, despite its evident needs. The monopolists of land and capital saw no way out of this dilemma but an aggressive search for foreign markets and outlets for capital investment.

To begin with, the chief trade rivals were England and Holland. In each of these countries an East India Company was formed with the object of exploiting the vast area of the Pacific Ocean between the Cape of Good Hope and Cape Horn; and the English and Dutch States bestowed on them full political, judicial and military powers, not only to claim and defend a monopoly of trade, but also to acquire territory. The inevitable result was a series of furious wars (1652-4, 1665-7 and 1673-4) in which the English were in the end victorious, only to resume a similar series in the following century, this time against the French.

The earlier part of the seventeenth century saw various foreign powers, namely the Holy Roman Emperor, the Grand Turk, and the English, Dutch, French and Swedish States, all making overtures to the Tsar that were connected with these new trends. Some wanted him as an ally against their rivals, and others commercial privileges, or permission to use the overland route to trade directly with Persia. These proposals were not regarded favourably; for the Russian ruling classes were beginning already to have ideas of their own about foreign markets, and had no wish for Russia to become someone else's. Perhaps, even then, they were dreaming of a time when their successors would be glad to have both Persia and Turkey as fields for economic expansion. The dream began to become a reality in the reign of Peter the Great (1689-1725), who spent seven years of subjection to a regency (1682-9) in studying the mechanical arts of the west, drilling troops and planning the creation of a great navy to open and maintain new trade routes to the south-west and north-west.

Since the White Sea is frozen for much of the year, the north-west trade route would depend absolutely on the attainment of a foothold on the shores of the Baltic. This was achieved after a war against Sweden lasting for more than twenty years, culminating in the annexation of Ingria, Karelia, Livonia, Esthonia and a part of Finland. Efforts at this time to establish the south-west route were unsuccessful; but Peter had begun his period of personal rule with a demonstration of the degree of force required to maintain autocratic rule. A military mutiny had been launched with the aim of replacing his mother as regent with his half-sister, who had previously been deposed. This happened while he was still abroad; and, by the time he reached home, the mutiny had been put down. He took a hand himself, however, in the trial and execution of more than 1,200 of the mutineers, some of whom he is said to have killed with his own hand.

The reign of Catherine II (1762-96) was notable for a domestic disturbance of a more fundamental nature. She had endeared herself to the upper ranks of society by introducing into Russia many of the refinements of western, particularly French, civilisation, but had done nothing even to alleviate the misery of the poor, let alone to investigate its cause. The result was a widespread insurrection, begun in 1773 by a Don Cossack named Pugachev. The insurgents, at any rate, had accurately identified the origins of their distress; for they lost no time in putting numerous landed proprietors to death. They also pillaged Kazan, and kept the whole country in a state of alarm for more than a year. In the end, Pugachev was caught and executed, but survived in written records and the collective memory to provide Tolstoy with one of his favourite examples of popular revolt suppressed by state force.

It was also during this reign that the objective of a trade route to the south-west was achieved. Alarmed by signs that the Russians were once more on the move westwards, the French incited the Turks to attack from the south. They declared war in 1768, but were defeated and forced not only to cede Azov, Kinburn and all the fortified places of the Crimea, but also to open the Bosphorus and the Dardanelles to Russian merchant vessels, so giving them access to the Mediterranean. A subsequent ambitious plan, made in concert with the Emperor Joseph II of Austria, to conquer and divide Turkey, was only partly successful. The Austrians were defeated; so the Russians, though victorious, had to be content with minor gains. The main prize, Constantinople, remained in Turkish hands, and was so to continue until the present day. Expansion westwards was continued, however, with the three partitions of Poland (1772, 1793 and 1795), and the annexation of Courland in 1795.

South-westerly expansion was to resume in the nineteenth century under the influence of increased economic pressures, and facilitated by new means of communication. It was during the reign of the Tsar Nicholas I (1825-55) that manufacturing industry was beginning to expand, enhancing the need for foreign trade that has already been noted. The army and the navy were growing commensurately with the new demands on them; and the construction of railways and canals, for the movement of both goods and troops, was well under way. The old kingdom of Georgia had been annexed at the beginning of the reign of the Tsar Alexander I (1801-25); and the Persian provinces of Erivan and Nakhichevan were to follow in 1826. Then began the long-drawn-out subjugation of the Caucasus, in which the young Tolstoy was to take part, and transmute his experience into the stories *The Raid, The Cossacks, The Woodfelling* and *Meeting an Acquaintance in the Detachment.*

Furthermore, under pretext of protecting the Christian population of the Ottoman Empire, Nicholas I obtained, by war or the threat of war, the autonomy of Moldavia, Wallachia and Serbia, the cession of several frontier districts together with the islands at the mouth of the Danube, and full liberty for Russian navigation and commerce in the Black Sea. Continued aggression was checked in 1831 by European intervention, and even more decively in 1854-6, when British and French armies landed in the Crimea and pursued a successful siege of Sevastopol, in the defence of which Tolstoy took part as an artillery officer.

Social change in mid-nineteenth century Russia was geared

to the material needs of the new industries and railways. The monopolists of land and capital demanded cheap labour for their factories; and it is probable that the labour-intensive steam railway could never have been run without it except as a non-profit-making public service. The economic restraint imposed on such landless wage-earners by the absence of any unappropriated land for them to go to would make any further legal restraint unnecessary. So it is fair to assume that the abolition of serfdom in 1861 owed less to changes of heart than to changing economic conditions. Details of the way in which the abolition was carried out support this view.

In the first place, the land was divided roughly into two, one half remaining with the landowners and the other being conditionally allocated to the peasants, who therefore held much less than they had actually cultivated before. In the second place, the peasants were allotted the worst land, which was assessed at a high price. In the third place, the forest lands on which they had been accustomed to rely for timber and fuel were normally assigned to the landowner. For their new holdings the peasants had to pay an annual rent ranging from eight to twelve roubles. As an alternative, they could work on their former owners' land for a fixed term – forty days a year for men, and thirty for women. These obligations could be redeemed by means of a state loan on which interest at the rate of six per cent was payable for a term of forty-nine years. It is therefore hardly surprising that all but the very wealthiest peasants found themselves engaged in a continual struggle against debt, and were obliged, in order to survive, either to perform extra work for the landlords for a low rate of pay, or to join the pool of cheap labour represented by the urban proletariat.

In the circumstances, it was natural that there should be considerable dissatisfaction and unrest among a rural population that had always tended to believe that, though they personally belonged to the landowners, the land itself, despite all theories to the contrary, belonged to them. As a corollary to this, they had also imagined in their innocence that, on the abolition of serfdom, this belief of theirs would be accepted and acted on by the State. The unrest among the peasants was at least equalled by that among the factory workers in the towns. Rural handicrafts had given way with alarming swiftness to mass production organised by managements with little concern for anything but a quick return for their outlay. It was said that, as a result, more people were killed and injured each year in Russian factories than during the entire Russo-Turkish war of 1877-8.

The situation was ripe for change, and afforded generous scope for Tolstoy to develop his ideas both on the State and on economic and social reform. He did not reach a positive and workable conclusion about the latter until some time after he had made up his mind about the State.

Chapter 6
Violent life of the State

Political power grows out of the barrel of a gun.
Mao Tse-tung.

H ENRI TROYAT, a Russian by birth and a Frenchman
by adoption, has given us a vivid description of what
must have been a turning-point in Tolstoy's life, when, during a
visit to Paris in 1857, seeking as ever for material to transmute
into literature, he went to watch a public execution.

Tolstoy was already familiar with death in many forms. For
two and a half years up to the end of 1853, first as a civilian
observer, then as a soldier, he had been present at what would
later be described as a 'mopping-up operation' still in progress
in the old kingdom of Georgia after its annexation by the Tsar
Alexander I in 1801. Then, on the outbreak of war with Turkey
in 1853, occasioned by the disintegration of the Ottoman
Empire and Russian ambitions in the Balkans, he was present,
first at the siege of Silistra, then, when this was raised in 1854,
on the invasion of the Crimea by British and French armies, at
the far more horrendous one of Sevastopol, lasting until 1856. It
was during this latter conflict that his initially favourable
attitude to war underwent some change.[1]

Despite all this, he was profoundly shocked by the execution.
The atrocities he had seen committed during the war in
moments of passion were far outdone by this cool, refined
and deliberate ending of a life. That very same day, he wrote to
his friend Vasily P. Botkin:

> The truth is that the State is a plot, designed not only to exploit but also
> to corrupt its citizens. For me, the laws laid down by politics are sordid
> lies .... I shall never enter the service of any government anywhere.[2]

36

Public executions, or indeed any executions at all, may be described with some justification as a corrupting influence; and Tolstoy, in using the word 'exploit', made a fair assessment of the activities pursued by the Russian and other ruling classes over the centuries. Nevertheless, he was to relax this resolution somewhat in 1861, when he accepted an appointment as 'arbiter of the peace' to settle disputes between serfs and landowners when the former ceased to be the private property of the latter. All the same, he did so with the excellent motive of ensuring that the serfs in his district were not cheated even of the meagre entitlement to land that the new law of emancipation allowed them. He thereby also ensured his personal unpopularity with his fellow-landlords, who made numerous complaints against him, and brought about his dismissal on the ground of 'ill-health'.

The anarchic sentiment that had prompted his letter to Botkin was to stay with him for the rest of his life, and to permeate everything that he wrote, particularly after his crisis of 1879. It seemed to him then that all his previous life had been wasted; and probably all that saved him from suicide was the working out of his personal religious convictions.

The South African War (1899-1902) provided both him and Aylmer Maude with material for intensive thought about the interests behind the power of the State. The discovery of gold in the Boer republics of the Transvaal and the Orange Free State had brought about an influx of British prospectors, who, when they became established, resented the taxes they had to pay, and demanded rights of citizenship that the Boers were slow to concede. That their ultimate intention was to run the countries in their own interests instead of those of the farmers was made plain by the Jameson Raid of 1895, an attempt to seize the Transvaal by a *coup de main*. When, after this, the British began to send troops to defend what they considered to be their commercial interests, the Boer republics decided on what would now be called a 'pre-emptive strike', and declared war on the 12th October 1899.

Maude quotes Tolstoy as having written to a Russian correspondent that he could not accept the prevailing view that all the blame for what followed could be attributed to one side or the other, but that the underlying causes of the conflict needed to be examined. He then went on:

> These causes, both in this Transvaal war and in all recent wars, are quite apparent to every man who does not shut his eyes. The causes are three: First, the unequal distribution of property, i.e. the robbing of some men by others; secondly, the existence of a military class, i.e. of people educated and fore-appointed to murder; and thirdly, the false, and for the most part consciously misleading religious teaching in which the young are compulsorily educated.[3]

He deplored the tendency to put all the responsibilty on 'Chamberlains and Wilhelms', who are 'but the blind tools of forces lying far beyond them', and proceeded to define these forces:

> As long as we make use of privileged wealth while the mass of the people are crushed by toil, there will always be wars for markets and for gold-mines, etc., which we need to maintain privileged wealth.

This analysis not only conforms to what we have already observed, but also was to receive striking confirmation after the First World War by an American researcher[4] who traced imperialism, and by inference imperialist wars, back to surplus manufactures and surplus capital requiring sale and investment abroad. But, as he would probably have agreed, if the home population had been receiving in wages the equivalent of their input of labour, no such surpluses would have existed. Poverty therefore causes war, which in turn, rather more obviously, causes more poverty.

Tolstoy's condemnation then continues to include with members of the armed forces, the instruments of war, the clergy who condone it. Tolstoy's use of the pronoun 'we' emphasizes his view that a better state of affairs will come about only when everybody understands the part that he or she plays in maintaining the existing one, if only by acquiescing in it.

Five years after the start of the South African War, another one nearer home prompted him to further protests, this time against the rulers of his own country. Russian business organisations had found it expedient to establish themselves in Manchuria and Korea, and had exerted pressure on the authorities to refuse to enter into negotiations with the Japanese for the purpose of setting up separate spheres of influence in these countries. Without declaring war, the Japanese attacked Port Arthur and rapidly defeated the Russians, by land at Mukden and by sea at Tsushima. Peace was re-established by the Treaty of Portsmouth (U.S.A.) in the following year, 1905.

Tolstoy's reaction was immediate. What, he demanded, had the material motives behind this war to do with the great majority of the Russian people?

> If there is a God, He will not ask me when I die (which may happen at any moment) whether I retained Chinnampo *with its timber stores,* or Port Arthur, or even that conglomeration which is called the Russian Empire, which he did not entrust to my care.[5]

Then again:

> For other people's land, to which the Russians have no right, *which has been stolen from its legitimate owners* and which in reality the Russians do not need – as well as *for certain shady dealings undertaken by speculators who wished to make money out of other people's forests* – enormous sums are spent, that is, a great part of the labour of the whole Russian people, while future generations of that people are being bound by debts, its best workmen withdrawn from labour, *and scores of thousands of its sons doomed to death.*[6]

And for good measure:

> And they know that the war is carried on not for anything at all necessary for the Russian people, but on account of *dealings in*

some alien 'leased land' (as they call it) *where it seemed advantageous to some contractors to build a railway* and engage on other affairs for profit.[7]

The indictment was a clear one. Firstly, there was robbery, both by support of the unequal distribution of property, and by taxation and public loans. Taxation takes from working people now alive a high proportion of the results of their labour, while the interest on public loans is a burden, not only on the present generation of workers, but also on generations yet to come. Secondly, there was the murder of thousands of young men sent to kill and be killed in a cause that did not concern them. But war is not the only reason for permanent armies.

In 1893, six years before the beginning of these events, Tolstoy had written at length[8] on the use of armed forces, not against those of a foreign country, but domestically, for the same purpose of maintaining 'privileged wealth'. In the late summer of 1892, he had been travelling by rail on a mission of famine relief to the Tula and Ryazan provinces, when he had encountered a special train carrying a punitive expedition to one of the estates where the peasants were starving. The troops were commanded by the provincial governor, and were armed, not only with rifles and ammunition, but also with rods for the infliction of floggings.

This was what had happened. The peasants had been tending a wood on land that they held in common with the landowner. They therefore considered the wood to be theirs, either wholly or in part; but the landowner assumed that it was his, and began to have the trees cut down. The peasants thereupon lodged a formal complaint with the courts. Both the governor and the public prosecutor assured Tolstoy that the peasants were in the right; but, despite this, the judge who first heard the case decided in favour of the landowner. All the higher courts, including the Senate, confirmed this decision; so the landowner ordered the felling of trees to be resumed. The peasants, however, unable to accept that the law could be manipulated in this unjust manner, refused to submit, and drove away the men who had been sent to carry out the work. When the matter was reported to the authorities at Petersburg, they ordered the governor to see that the decision of the courts was obeyed. It was the troops sent for this purpose that Tolstoy happened to meet.

He was well aware of the standard procedure on these occasions: it had recently been used at Orel. If the peasants were to persist in their resistance, and ignore a warning volley fired over their heads, they would be fired upon in earnest until they dispersed. Any of those remaining alive who had been seen to resort to violence themselves would be tried by a special military tribunal and hanged. If, on the other hand, the peasants were to disperse peacefully, a number of them would be designated, without any form of trial, as 'ringleaders', and flogged with rods on their bare backs. Seventy strokes had been the number awarded at Orel; but a man would probably be unconscious after fifty.

How, Tolstoy then proceeded to wonder, could men whom he knew in ordinary life to be individually honest and kindly assume the responsibility for, or carry out, acts of such monstrous cruelty? These are the answers that he proposed, in terms that still ring true today:

> Those in authority who have initiated and abetted and directed the affair will say that they act as they do because such things are necessary for the maintenance of the existing order and the maintenance of the existing order is necessary for the welfare of the country, for humanity, and for the possibility of social existence and human progress.
>
> Men of the lower orders – the peasants and soldiers who have to execute this violence with their own hands – will say that they do so because it is ordered by the higher authorities and higher authorities know what they are doing. And it appears to them an indubitable truth that the right people constitute authority, and that they know what they are doing. If they admit the possibility of mistakes or errors they do so only in regard to officials of lower rank. The highest power, on whom everything depends, seems to them unquestionably infallible.

In Tula, in the late summer of 1892, however, events took a different turn from the ones at Orel. Some of the bystanders at the railway station, including, one may well imagine, Tolstoy himself, together with some of the prospective participants in the affair, expressed in no uncertain terms their indignation at the action that was contemplated; and the soldiers in the end did no more than finish cutting down the wood. The robbery was consummated, but neither the murder nor the torture. This achievement of a peaceful solution to a particular incident was a sample of Tolstoy's idea of a general solution to the whole human predicament.

The State, he said, must go – not just the Russian State, but all States. They may have been useful once for protecting people from violence; but, by the end of the nineteenth century, they were initiating more violence than they prevented. Had he lived another four years, and seen the events of 1914, he would certainly have been confirmed in this opinion.

The method by which they should be induced to go was another matter. Further violence was out of the question; for a new order so set up would be obliged to maintain itself in precisely the same manner as the old. In any case, the use of violence was contrary to Christ's fourth commandment. Here Tolstoy incurred the scorn of Lenin,[9] who contrasted the critic of 'capitalist exploitation', 'government outrages' and the simultaneous spread of great wealth and great poverty with the 'crackpot' preacher of 'resist not evil'.

History was to prove Tolstoy right and Lenin wrong. Tolstoy was right in the sense that violence was not the answer; but only the future will tell whether his own idea will ever work. It coincides with one proposed in mid-16th century by a Frenchman, Etienne de la Boétie, who wrote:

Ce sont les peuples mêmes qui se laissent ou plutôt se font gour-mander, puisqu'en cessant de servir ils en seraient quittes. C'est le peuple qui s'asservit, qui se coupe la gorge: qui, ayant le choix d'être sujet ou d'être libre, quitte sa franchise et prend le joug: qui consent à son mal ou plutôt le pourchasse.[10]

It is the peoples themselves who allow themselves to be, or rather have themselves, gobbled up; for, in ceasing to serve, they would be rid of it all. It is the people who enslave themselves, who cut their own throats: who, having the choice to be subject or to be free, abandon their freedom and take up the yoke: who consent to their own misfortune or rather chase after it.

Tolstoy was later[11] to quote la Boétie at length; but the theory had been implicit in his own thought for some time. Deprived of its soldiers, police, lawyers, judges, gaolers and civil servants, no State could function. All that was necessary was for enough people to make up their minds as he himself had done in 1857:

I shall never enter the service of any government anywhere.

Tolstoy's general sympathy for the mass of mankind would probably have been enough on its own to account for his attitude to rulers; but it is also likely that an incident that occurred to him personally in July 1862 gave some extra vivacity to his expression of it.[12]

A school that he had started on his own for the benefit of peasants' children had become popular enough for him to set up more and enlist the help of a few students, one of whom was under police surveillance for having circulated revolutionary tracts. Tolstoy himself had been suspect ever since his period of office as 'arbiter of the peace', during which, in the opinion of the authorities, he had shown too much favour to the peasants.

A body of armed police, therefore, taking advantage of his absence on a cure by the banks of the River Karalyk, descended in force on his home, surrounded it to forestall escapes, and carried out a comprehensive search. They ran through his manuscripts, read his private diary and letters, making a note of the names of his correspondents, broke locks, and tore off curtain linings. Outside, they prised up flagstones and dragged the ponds. Finding nothing, because his aunt and sister had managed to hide some material that would have got him into trouble, they extended the search to the schools, seized the children's notebooks and arrested the student helpers. Still they found nothing. It must have been immediately obvious to the police that the raid had been a mistake; and they probably regretted it still more when Tolstoy, in his wrath, used the influence of a distant relative at court to extract half an apology from the governor of Tula. This experience, exacerbated by subsequent conflicts with the censor, was one that Tolstoy was not likely to forget.

Another, which he certainly remembered for the rest of his life, with both detestation for the authorities responsible and remorse for his own part in it, was the trial and execution in 1866 of a private soldier called Vasili Shabunin. It has provided sufficient material for a whole book.[13] Tolstoy was called upon by two military acquaintances to defend this soldier, who stood accused of the military crime of striking an officer. He agreed to do so, but had no means of knowing that a falsified version of the events leading up to the incident was going to be presented at the trial. In fact, the officer, Captain Yasevich, had taken a report that Shabunin had copied for him, crumpled it and thrown it in his face. Had the trial proceeded on this basis, the punishment would probably have been exile to Siberia; but reasons of state, quite unconnected with this particular affair, were behind the official intention to take stronger measures.

Earlier in the same year, an attempt had been made to assassinate the Tsar Alexander II, who forthwith began to imagine a widespread conspiracy against him. Perhaps there was; but there was no reason for anybody to believe that Shabunin had any part in it. Nevertheless, it was expedient that he should die as an example; so a falsified account of his crime was composed, according to which the only provocation he had suffered was a reprimand for being late on parade. Tolstoy, in his speech for the defence, referred to the true provocation; but the court ignored what he said. His subsequent petition to the Tsar was delayed, on the feeble ground of his failure to quote the number of the regiment, until after the execution by firing squad had been carried out.

Tolstoy's plea had been one of diminished responsibility owing to mental weakness and the influence of alcohol; and, in later life, he reproached himself for having based it on man-made laws and regulations instead of on eternal principles of right and wrong. He could hardly have imagined that such an approach to the problem would have had any more immediate success than the one he in fact adopted. Shabunin was lost in any case; but so was an opportunity to publicise the cruel injustices inherent in state proceedings.

Chapter 7
The verdict of history

As long as war is regarded as wicked, it will always have its fascination. When it is looked upon as vulgar, it will cease to be popular.
Oscar Wilde.

WHEREVER it was that Tolstoy acquired his information about the commercial reasons for British military operations in South Africa, and for the Russian presence in Manchuria that led to the Russo-Japanese War, he was certainly well informed. The American researcher to whom reference has already been made, namely Parker Thomas Moon, Associate Professor of International Relations in the University of Columbia, elaborated on both themes, and confirms Tolstoy's views in every respect. Here he is on the subject of the background to the Boer War:

From Rhodesia, the greatest achievement of Cecil Rhodes, we must turn our attention to the Boer communities of Transvaal and Orange River. These, as we have seen, had been recognized as self-governing republics, and had been left to pursue their own interests, until with the discovery of gold in the northern republic, Transvaal, about the year 1886, a new factor entered into the situation. The thousands of prospectors, laborers, and tradesmen, who rushed into the Transvaal gold fields in the period after 1886, soon incurred the bitter hostility of the Boer farmers , who believed the land was theirs by right of conquest and settlement, and regarded the newcomers, with some cause, as a disorderly and dangerous element. The Boers, for their part, angered the miners by excluding them from political rights, by levying heavy tariff duties on food and other supplies, by establishing dynamite and railway monopolies which interfered with the miners' business.[1]

So far it would seem that there were faults on both sides; but Moon goes on to describe the need of the mine-owners for native labour, and their belief that the latter should be forced to work for them by means of taxation or otherwise. He illustrates this by quoting the words of one of them, a man by the name of Rudd:

> If under the cry of civilization we in Egypt lately mowed down ten or twenty thousand dervishes with Maxims [he was referring to the battle of Omdurman, surely it cannot be considered a hardship to compel the natives in South Africa to give three months in the year to do a little honest work.[2]

But the Boers interfered with the importation of native labour. There followed the unsuccessful Jameson Raid of 1895 (Ch.6), which the British cabinet effectively disowned.As time went on, however, they were more and more impelled to preparations for war for reasons that Moon goes on to explain:

> ... First and foremost, the British mining interests in Transvaal were dissatisfied with the Boer government because, representing the interests of the Boer farmers as opposed to British industrialists, it levied tariff duties on food, compelled British mining companies to buy dynamite and coal at exorbitant prices from monopolies, balked all attempts to establish convenient railway communications with the Cape, permitted the debauching of native laborers by saloons, and, in general, as Mr Hays Hammond so admirably explained, *reduced the profits of the mine-owners by twelve millions a year.*[3]

This, of course, was not the reason alleged for the break. What was alleged was the far safer one of the franchise, from which newcomers were excluded for a period of fourteen years. A five year period of qualification is generally regarded as being a justifiable one, and Kruger in the end offered seven; but Sir Alfred Milner, High Commissioner for South Africa, regarded anything more than five as putting British citizens in the Transvaal 'in the position of helots'. He also said that 'the only effective way of protecting our subjects is to help them to cease to be our subjects'. Moon comments as follows:

> ... Patriotism ordinarily dictates the opposite course, the retention of subjects, and the reader may perhaps wonder why a nation should be willing to fight in order to 'protect' subjects so unpatriotic as to desire citizenship in another nation. But the paradox is easily explained if one remembers that underneath the superficial franchise question *lay the fundamental economic reason why Englishmen desired power in Transvaal, and the imperialist desire for dominant power in all South Africa.*[4]

Even the imperialist Colonial Secretary, Joseph Chamberlain, was willing to consider Kruger's offer; but Milner talked him round. Then, when Kruger was willing to forego the crucial two years, Milner found other grievances, and British military preparations went ahead. Troops began to be moved to South Africa from India and the Mediterranean, while an expeditionary force was assembled in England. There was nothing left for the Boers to do but to take the initiative or submit to occupation.

In case it should be imagined that Moon's description of the foundation of Rhodesia as 'the greatest achievement of Cecil Rhodes' is meant to be taken at its face value, a brief account of how it was done is in order. The country to the north of Bechuanaland and the Transvaal was known to be fertile and well-watered, and, though within the tropics, to be high enough for European occupation. It was inhabited by the Matabeles and the Mashonas under King Lo Bengula. In order to forestall the Portuguese, Rhodes first sent a British missionary to induce the king to sign a treaty that amounted to a first option for British entrepreneurs. This done, he sent three of his most trusted lieutenants, Rudd, Maguire and Thompson, to arrange a 'mineral concession' giving them 'complete and exclusive charge over all metals and minerals situated and contained in my kingdom, principalities and dominions', together with the right 'to exclude from my kingdom, etc., all persons seeking land, metals, minerals, or mining rights therein'. The document was signed on the 30th October 1888.

In return for all this, Lo Bengula was to receive one thousand Martini rifles, a hundred thousand rounds of ammunition and one hundred pounds a month. The negotiators also gratified his wish for a steamboat by giving him a second-hand one into the bargain. His innocent trust is illustrated by a message he sent later to Queen Victoria:

> Some time ago a party of men came into my country, the principal one appearing to be a man called Rudd. They asked me for a place to dig gold and said they would give me certain things for the right to do so. I told them to bring what they would and I would show them what I would give. A document was written and presented to me for signature. *I asked what it contained and was told that in it were my words and the words of those men.* I put my hand to it. About three months afterwards I heard from other sources that I had given by that document the right to all the minerals of my country.[5]

He had given even more without knowing it. Rhodes interpreted the concession as giving him not only 'metals and minerals', but also the right to rule and exploit generally.

With this in mind, he organised a company (the British South Africa Company, and applied to the British authorities at home for a charter. The Prime Minister, Lord Salisbury, at first had doubts about this; but Rhodes won him over by inviting the Duke of Abercorn to become the company's President, and the Duke of Fife to become Vice-President. He also stated that 'the conditions of the natives inhabiting the said territories will be materially improved and their civilization advanced'. The charter, signed on the 29th October 1889, gave the South Africa Company the right, for twenty-five years, to 'make treaties and laws, maintain police, construct roads, railways and harbors, develop mines and industries, make grants of land, and, in short, govern a vast *but purposely undefined area,* north of British Bechuanaland and Transvaal, and west of Portuguese

Mozambique, but with no northern boundary'.

The fraud had worked well enough, but, when the actual settlement was resisted, armed force had to be used, and Lo Bengula, like the man who admitted the camel's foot into his tent, was driven out. What had been his kingdom came to be known as Rhodesia.

Tolstoy's already quoted comments on the Russo-Japanese War, waged 'on account of dealings in some alien "leased land" (as they call it) where it seemed advantageous to some contractors to build a railway and engage on other affairs for profit' are a reference to the events that followed the Sino-Japanese War of 1894-1895, in which European-trained Japanese troops had defeated the ill-organised Chinese. The most important provision of the resulting treaty of Shimonoseki was the session to Japan of the Liaotung Peninsula, the southern tip of Manchuria, commanding the entry to the Gulf of Chih-li and Peking.

This intrusion on their own 'spheres of influence' in China was more than the authorities of Russia, Germany and France could stand; so they sent a joint note, with which the Japanese complied, 'advising' that Japan should refrain from annexing any part of the Chinese mainland. It must not be imagined that the three States acted as they did out of any spirit whatsoever of altruistic chivalry: indeed, they expected and obtained compensation, of which the Russian share was as follows.

The Chinese statesman Li Hung Chang was persuaded the following year, after a visit to Russia, to authorise a 'Russo-Chinese Bank', financed largely with French capital, with the task of helping the Chinese to pay their war indemnity to Japan, and, more important from the Russian point of view, *that of acquiring concessions for the construction of railways and telegraphs*. In the September of the same year, it obtained such a concession, and a very important one. A 'Chinese Eastern Railway' was to connect the Russian Trans-Siberian Railway with the terminus of Vladisvostok. Instead of going by a circuitous route through Russian territory, it would go straight across the Manchurian provinces of China. The right of way was to be free; and railway property and receipts were to be exempt from taxation. The company's bonds were to be *guaranteed by the Russian State.*

This last clause in the agreement emphasised that the venture was not a purely business one. In the event of war, the railway would provide for more expeditious troop movements; and, even in peacetime, Russian military units, posted along the line to guard it from attack, would ensure Russian domination of Manchuria. As a matter of course, possession of the railway would carry with it a near monopoly of the commerce of central and northern Manchuria; but, in addition, the company was to have mining rights along the route. The next move was to obtain a concession for a southern extension of the line, with attendant mining rights, as far as the ice-free harbour of Port Arthur; but the war put an end to these aspirations to control southern as well as northern Manchuria.

The example we have quoted from Tolstoy of state-instigated violence against the home population is insignificant compared with what was to happen in 1905.[6] During the firing of a salute, a shot fell close to the Tsar Nicholas II, whereupon he decided to leave Moscow. Three days after this, a huge deputation of strikers and their families, led by a certain Father Gapon, marched to the Winter Palace. Although the crowd was unarmed, the troops were ordered to open fire; and many lives were lost. This was the signal for a peasant uprising throughout the country, in which manor-houses were attacked, police officers were assassinated, and the Grand Duke Serge, uncle of the Tsar, was murdered in Moscow. It was then at last realised at Court that the time had come for some concessions to be made. Reforms were announced affecting dissenters, Jews and the subject peoples; and the censorship of the press was allowed to lapse. Finally, a consultative Duma, or parliament, was established, though chosen by indirect election. Pobedonostsev, Minister to the Holy Synod, who had been the Tsar's tutor, and had influenced him greatly in the direction of coercion rather than conciliation, was dismissed. As the next chapter will show, a British critic of Tolstoy's political ideas does not hesitate to claim that it was this policy of coercion that kept the revolution at bay for another twelve years; but a more liberal view would be that it was the reforms, limited though they were.

This is not the place to give more than a sample of the imperialist activities that so disturbed Tolstoy; but probably the most comprehensive account of those that occurred since about 1875 is to be found in Moon's book.[1] They conform to the same pattern as the ones here described. After a careful perusal of them, it is hard to see how any fair-minded reader could do other than pronounce Tolstoy right in his conclusions, however contrary they may be to history as commonly taught in schools..

He was not alone in his opinions. At about the same period, Anatole France was ironically describing the origin of private property in land in his colony of penguins turned into human beings. A giant penguin has clubbed a little one to death, saying, 'Your field belongs to me!' The holy man Maël, cause of the transformation, calls this act murder and robbery, but is reproved as follows by the monk Bulloch:

'Prenez garde, mon père', dit Bulloch avec douceur, 'que ce que vous appelez le meurtre et le vol est en effet la guerre et la conquête, fondements sacrés des empires et sources de toutes les vertus et de toutes les grandeurs humaines'.[7]

Take care, Father', said Bulloch gently, 'lest what you call murder and robbery are not in reality war and conquest, the sacred foundations of empires, and the sources of all human virtue and greatness.

Now that the end of the twentieth century is not far off, and so much has happened to justify these views of Tolstoy, one is disappointed to come across evidence that there are still people who believe that actions condemned as criminal in private individuals belong to a different category when performed by the State. Here, for example, is an extract from the guide to Holy Trinity Church, Blythburgh, Suffolk :

The church plate was handed over to John Hopton by King Henry VIII when he dissolved the Priory. ... In Tudor times new plate was purchased. That too was lost, *this time by theft*. (Author's italics).

Chapter 8
Tolstoy on the State: the critical assessment

Politicians make strange bedfellows, but they all share the same bunk.
Edgar A. Shoaff.

T OLSTOY'S severe verdict on state morality led, as was inevitable, to criticism, some supportive, but on the whole adverse. The critic supremely well placed to form an opinion about him was his friend and translator Aylmer Maude, who, during Tolstoy's lifetime, and while they were still in constant touch with one another, appears on the whole to have shared his views. For example, he produces with approval the following quotation from Thoreau:

> I heartily accept the motto – 'That Government is best which governs least'; and I should like to see it acted up to more rapidly and systematically. Carried out, it finally amounts to this, which also I believe – 'That Government is best which governs not at all'; and when men are prepared for it, that will be the kind of Government which they will have ... .[1]

Thoreau's remedy, in line with Tolstoy's and la Boétie's, was non-cooperation and failure to pay taxes; but Maude is at pains to point out that, although Tolstoy was 'in good company' in this matter, and was offering 'just what some people pine for: something definite and decided to do or to refuse to do, ...',[2] he was really more interested in the idea that 'progress in human well-being can only be achieved by relying more and more on reason and conscience and less and less on man-made laws'.[3]

54

But, if your 'reason and conscience' tell you that a man-made law is wrong, how can you follow them except by ignoring the law? One senses here a subconscious wish to deviate from Tolstoy's strong line, but some uncertainty about how to do it. All the same, Maude does not attempt to deny that 'injustice and inequality' are 'flagrant among us today'.[4]

He was more ready to be definite where his own empire was concerned, as for example in the following passage aimed at the British presence in India:

> Our pretence that we murder and steal in order to do good to less civilised nations, amounts to a declaration that the best results are obtainable, not by doing right but by doing wrong, and that as a nation we have reached a state of civilisation which we are prepared to force upon others.[5]

He does not, however, single out the wrong-doers, but, by his use of the first person plural, appears to accept a share of the responsibility for their wrong-doing.

This was his attitude in 1902. Six years later, when the first part of his biography of Tolstoy was published, he was beginning to find reasons for Tolstoy's opinions on the State other than that of their correctness. For example:

> His unsatisfactory experience of administrative work [i.e. in his post of 'arbiter of the peace' in 1861] perhaps increased the anti-Governmental bias shown in his later works.[6]

Here the attempt to find a personal explanation for opinions of universal significance, and the use of the pejorative term 'bias', indicate a distinct change of front. Perhaps too, Maude thought, these opinions could have had a literary origin:

> Like Rousseau, it suited him better to reform the world on paper, or even to alter his own habits of life, than to concern himself with the slow social progress, the bit-by-bit amelioration, which alone is possible to those harnessed to the car that bears a whole society of men.[7]

And why not? There is room in this world for both the bit-by-bit improvers, of whom there are many, and for the men of useful innovatory ideas, of whom there has always been a painful shortage. Furthermore, without the ideas of the latter, it is hard to imagine what the former would do, except move in many different, perhaps opposed, directions. Before Rousseau,[8] it was generally assumed that a political community pretending to sovereignty derived the authority of its laws from its rulers or from its magistracy. After Rousseau, fewer and fewer believed that it derived this authority other than from itself. So far, practice has not risen to the heights of this theory; but the theory is universal and true. Perhaps Tolstoy, who was thoroughly familiar with Rousseau's works, saw himself as engaged in a similar task.

In the meantime, it is to be regretted that he is still far from being regarded in the same light as was Rousseau in the latter half of the eighteenth century. We have already noted (ch. 6) that the founder of the Russian Revolution, V.I. Lenin, regarded him with a curious mixture of admiration and contempt on account of what he saw as the 'contradictions' in his philosophy; but there is no doubt of his admiration of Tolstoy's denunciations of the State as then constituted:

> Tolstoi's indictment of the ruling classes was made with tremendous power and sincerity; with absolute clearness he laid bare the inner falsity of all those institutions by which modern society is maintained: the church, the law courts, militarism, 'lawful' wed-lock, bourgeois science.[9]

He then criticises Tolstoy for what he considers a failure to realise that the forces of tyranny could be overcome only by the proletariat's 'intelligent, consistent, thorough-going, implacable struggle against them'. He did not foresee, as Tolstoy did, that, as a result of this struggle, the Tsarist tyranny would be replaced by that of the Communist Party, under which not only would general conformity continue to be enforced, but also the lives of individuals would be shaped and directed in accordance with preconceived political theory.

A modern Soviet critic, Victor Shklovsky, gives the impression of treading warily so as not to expose himself to being criticised on the same grounds as Tolstoy had been by Lenin. His references to Tolstoy's opinions on the State are few and muted, but nevertheless indicate agreement. For example:

It was easier to sweep out one's room than to reshape the world. For the present Tolstoy was tidying and re-shaping his own quarters, not touching the children's rooms, but he was describing the injustice of the world with such exactness and was remoulding himself with such sincerity that he was a reproach to his time. In Russia, crushed by police terror after 1881, Tolstoy seemed to be knocking on all doors, saying: Do not sleep, the timbers are burning in your house, your destiny is smouldering. Retribution will come. The people around you are living in misery and it is you who have robbed them.[10]

And again:

The government itself, cruel and seemingly powerful, was becoming an illusion, a historical survival; the military might of Russia was also an illusion.[11]

The American Ernest J. Simmons, internationally recognised as a Tolstoy scholar, finds himself in two minds. Here is Simmons, counsel for the prosecution:

... Tolstoy, however much he may try, fails to resolve the central dilemma of his faith, which really did not exist for him although he knew it did for the majority of his readers. That is, on the basis of Christ's gospel of love, how can we live peacefully in this world of violence without requiring or enforcing laws or without meeting violence by violence? In short, can he be asking readers to surrender supinely to Stalins and Hitlers?[12]

And for the defence:

... To one cable from America as to whether he favored Russia or

Japan, he replied with his usual courage: 'I am neither for Russia nor Japan, but for the working people of both countries who have been deceived by their governments and forced to go to war against their own good, their conscience and their religion'.[13]

Here, had Simmons realised it, is the first step towards the answer to his question about Stalins and Hitlers.

Simmons also shares Tolstoy's lack of faith in disarmament conferences, and, by implication, in the States that send representatives to them:

> In fact, the question of disarmament which had originally inspired the Hague Conference of nations got nowhere, and scarcely before it had ended one of the participators, Britain, was engaged in the Boer War.[14]

It is a completely different story when we come to Henri Troyat, French but Russian-born:

> ... If everyone loved other people more than himself and the world were inhabited exclusively by followers of Leo Tolstoy, there would obviously be no need of laws, courts, police or government. ... If mere non-resistance could convince and ceasing to fight could convert, we might demobilize the army and throw open the frontiers.[15]

The Englishman Theodore Redpath writes in the same vein:

> Nor has Tolstoy proved anarchy desirable. He has not proved modern governments always or even generally worse than no government. ... And was it not states that abolished slavery, and established the rights of free speech and public meeting? And did not states sometimes protect the poor against the rich?[16]

A.N. Wilson is equally uncompromising:

> If Tolstoy had been involved in such a campaign as the wars against Napoleon and Hitler, in which so many heroic Russians

lost their lives for an observable end, he might have wanted to say that there were some circumstances in which war was the only solution to a case of international conflict.[17]

And on the subject of state violence against the home population:
It has to be said that the policy of repression of which Pobedonostsev was the architect worked. The Revolution was held off for another quarter century and more. And it could be argued that if the reactionaries had not given in in 1905, they would not have been caught off guard twelve years later by the comparatively small insurrection of the Bolshevics.[18]

These are specimens of what the critics say. Since what the friendly critics say merely confirms what has already been established in Chapter 7 by means of objective evidence, there should be no necessity for further comment. The others, however, need to be closely examined, to see whether their objections are relevant and valid.

We must first look at a tendency to avoid meeting Tolstoy on his own ground; in other words, to assume that he meant something different from what he actually said, and to concentrate on that. The honourable exception is Ernest J. Simmons, who, in citing the Russo-Japanese War, concedes that Tolstoy was on the side of both the Russian and Japanese working people, and against both States concerned. What a pity that he had already confused the issue by appealing to the instinct of human beings, or indeed animals of any species, to defend themselves when *individually* attacked!

The fact is that Tolstoy was the defender of the common man and woman wherever they were to be found, and against the rulers who both oppressed them and led them out to war against each other. To the question: 'What would you have done if you had found your country attacked by a Napoleon, a Hitler or a Stalin?', he might, in one of his occasional moods of patriotism, implanted in him by his upbringing, have replied: 'Fight!'. On the other hand, in a more thoughtful mood, he would probably have replied: 'I should have done what lay within my power to convince the alleged subjects of those men calling themselves emperors or dictators that they should think again, and refuse either to take oaths of allegiance to them, or to obey their orders to perform any immoral action'.

The same policy of evasion is evident in the assertion that Tolstoy had proved neither anarchy to be desirable, nor the results of state action to be worse than those of anarchy. But this is not the only complaint that has to be made against Dr Redpath; for it seems to have escaped his notice that Tolstoy himself expressly admitted that no such proof is possible:

> It cannot be proved, as the champions of the State affirm, that the abolition of the State would involve the social chaos, mutual robberies and murders, the destruction of all social institutions and a return of mankind to savagery. *Nor can it be proved, as opponents of government maintain, that men have already become so reasonable and good that they do not wish to rob and murder one another, but prefer peaceful intercourse to enmity, and will themselves arrange all that they need unaided by the State, and that therefore the State, far from being an aid, exercises a harmful and embittering influence under pretence of protecting people.* It is not possible by abstract reasoning to prove either of these contentions.[19]

He then pointed out that, even if our dependence on state protection at any given time should be conceded, the time will come when we shall outgrow this dependence, just as the chick outgrows its need for the protection of the eggshell. The State will then inevitably disappear.

As for States' having abolished slavery, there is little credit owing to them on that account; for they have done so under pressure, and when it was evident that there was a better way of robbing people of their rightful earnings. Tolstoy saw that depriving men of the land they need to work on not only takes away their freedom and reduces their wages just as effectively as does owning their bodies, but also involves fewer responsibilities. The abolition of serfdom in Russia, as we have seen, was followed by a general worsening of the former serfs' standard of living, simply because the total area of land available for their cultivation was approximately halved, and they had to pay for their highly assessed allotments by way of either rent or redemption of a state loan. Similarly in the United States of America, the negro slaves had no reason to be grateful for their emancipation; for the alternative offered to them, namely to work for their former owners for wages, brought about no essential alleviation of their plight. One important difference was that, whereas it was in the owners' interest to look after their slaves when there was a lack of work, employers had no such motive to retain the services of redundant wage-earners.

Even less credit is due for what Redpath sees as States' establishment of the rights of free speech and public meeting. All they did was restore what they themselves had taken away, that is to say, rights that have existed since the beginnings of speech, and indeed of communication of any sort whatsoever. Furthermore, anybody asking the rhetorical question whether States have not sometimes protected the poor against the rich should be asked to name a few examples. The English Court of Star Chamber certainly performed such a function; but it did not outlast the Great Rebellion.

Finally the plea that Pobedonostsev did a good job because he preserved the *status quo* for a few more years begs the question whether this result was so desirable that the most violent means justified its achievement. A saner view would be that any State whose unpopularity is such that its continued existence depends on force is one that has outlived any usefulness it may ever have had.

The pointlessness of much of the controversy of which we have here studied some examples will be better understood when once a clear distinction has been generally accepted between the State, to which Tolstoy objected on account of both its violent origins and its continuing exploitative purposes backed by violence, and 'government', a term whose usage in the sense of a body of people vested with legislative and executive authority has been intentionally avoided in the present work. The term 'government' may be more usefully employed in the sense of a system devised by a community, and operated by itself, for the purpose of preserving the freedom and security of its members as individuals.

Such a system, in the form of peasant assemblies in the *mir* (the village assembly) and the *volost* (the canton assembly), which, in 1861, were withdrawn from the jurisdiction of the landowners and reinvested with powers of self-government, would have been thoroughly familiar to Tolstoy; and, so far as we know, he had no objection to it. So, although as a disciple of Rousseau he may have thought that humanity, once freed from the State, would be absolved by its natural goodness from the need of any form of control, there is no reason to believe that he would have held rigidly to this view in the face of all arguments and experience. Further discussion on these matters will be postponed until we consider the significance of Tolstoy's philosophy for us today.

Chapter 9
The Golden Regiment

I reject get-it-done, make-it-happen thinking. I want to slow things down so I understand them better.
Governor Jerry Brown.

A CURIOUS observer of the Moscow of 1881, one generation after the emancipation of the serfs, would have marvelled at the proliferation of beggars. They were to be found in every street. Unlike the beggars of the countryside, who still made a confident appeal in the name of Christ, they would attempt to catch the eye of passers-by, and delay their plea until they thought they detected a look of sympathy. Large numbers of them would congregate outside churches when services were in progress, especially funeral services.

The diffident approach of these beggars had a simple explanation. What they were doing was against the law. Count Leo Tolstoy, who was one observer of the scene,[1] not merely curious but deeply concerned, saw one of them, ragged and 'swollen with dropsy', being pushed into a cab by a policeman. Anxious to know what was going to happen, he followed in another cab to the police station, which he entered on the heels of the beggar and the policeman. A man armed with a sword and a pistol, and seated behind a table, when asked by Tolstoy, 'What has that peasant been arrested for?', replied briefly with some embarrassment, 'The authorities order such people to be arrested, so it has to be done'. This was, and still is, the standard reaction everywhere of subordinate officials, on whom the State depends.

Tolstoy witnessed such incidents on several subsequent occasions. On one of them, as many as thirty were being escorted away by police, marching in the front and the rear of

63

the little crowd. From the police station, as he now knew, they would be taken to the Usupov workhouse. He was never able to fathom why, despite all this police activity, the number of beggars on the streets always appeared to be the same. Were some of them perhaps begging legally? Were new ones constantly appearing to take the places of those arrested? Or were there altogether too many for the police to deal with?

The year 1881 has been named specifically, because that was the year in which Tolstoy, for family reasons, moved for the time being from Yasnaya Polyana to Moscow. The poverty he found there shocked him profoundly, accustomed though he was to the sight of the rural variety, and set him off on his new career of world reformer. His psychological disposition had for a long time been such as to fit him for this rôle.

There is an early period in the life of us all when, surrounded with love and care by the only adult beings that we know, we assume ourselves to be the centre of all life and activity. Different people take varying times to emerge from this state, which, when perpetuated and extended to include a belief that the universe was meant for man, is known as the fallacy of the central position. Some people never emerge from it. Tolstoy, according to his own account of his first visit to Moscow, did so at the age of nine:

> For the first time I envisaged the idea that we – that is, our family – were not the only people in the world, that not every conceivable interest was centred in ourselves but that there existed another life – that of people who had nothing in common with us, cared nothing for us, had no idea of our existence even. I must have known all this before but I had not known it as I did now – I had not realized it; I had not felt it.[2]

Instead of forgetting about these people, he showed precocious originality by beginning to wonder how they lived, what they lived on, and how they brought up their children.

Now, in 1881, the mature Tolstoy, faced with the grim problem of the Moscow beggars, began in earnest to search for the solution, symbolised by the writing on the 'green stick' of his brother Nicholas, to all the ills of the world.

When he spoke about these matters to his Muscovite acquaintances, he was told that what he had already seen was nothing compared with what he would see in the dosshouses at Khitrov market. That was where he could inspect the so-called 'Golden Company', or rather, as one humorist put it, the 'Golden Regiment', their numbers had swollen so much of late. In Tolstoy's opinion, 'army' was the right word for the people whose numbers he was later to estimate at 50,000. Several times he set off for Khitrov market, but was turned back by a sense of shame at going to look at people he could not help. It must have been the same feeling that caused his concern at the reaction to this social problem of the high society in which he moved. They seemed to him to be proud of knowing about it, just as London high society had seemed to be proud of knowing about the London poor when he visited England twenty years before. Nevertheless, in the end he went to see for himself, not only at Khitrov market, but also at the Rzhanov fortress and elsewhere.

Most of the inhabitants of these places, he found, were working people, contented and cheerful for the most part, though living in cramped and insanitary conditions. Categories more disturbing to his peace of mind consisted of those who had come down in the world, and were therefore alien to the dosshouse existence, and prostitutes, whose way of life seemed to have become a permanent and accepted feature of society.

His first reactions, he admitted, were self-centred and emotional. Guilt came first, then satisfaction, induced by his friends' praise, with his own goodness in feeling guilty, and then a feeling that this poverty was not a result of his own luxurious way of living, but was an inevitable condition of life. As a way, therefore, both of exhibiting his own goodness and of benefiting the destitute, he decided to organise some measures of practical relief. It so happened that a census was due at that time; so he planned, with the assistance of those participating in it, who were mostly students, to make an assessment of the needs of individuals, and to help them with money, with finding work, or, if appropriate, with getting back to their villages. Children were to be found places in schools, and old folk in almshouses.

He proposed to raise the necessary funds by canvassing his rich friends; but here he came across an unforeseen difficulty. Those who prided themselves on their philanthropy were already committed. Ladies were dressing little dolls, at minimal expense to themselves compared with their luxurious clothes and furnishings, and offering them for raffles to raise money for the poor. Gentlemen would make donations in consideration of grants of honours from the State; but they had already received all the existing ones, and the State was reluctant to institute any more. Tolstoy received numerous vague promises, but no hard cash, except from the students working on the census. To complete his embarrassment, he discovered that all the applications for financial help were from people who had come down in the world, and wanted to go back up again.

Realising at last that his scheme of relief was useless, he began to consider seriously why it was that such poverty existed. If the cause could be removed, then the effect should disappear. The first question he asked himself was why peasants should leave the country for the town. The obvious answer was that otherwise they would be unable to provide themselves with enough food. Too much of the wealth they produced went in taxes to the State and in rent to the landowner. This was a process amounting to 'the passing of wealth from the producers into the hands of non-producers'.[3] So these producers, who are for this reason unable to gain a livelihood by carrying on with their traditional tasks, migrate to the towns, where the non-producers congregate to enjoy their idle life under police protection. There the migrants either perform menial work for the non-producers, or occupy the lowlier positions in industry and trade.

So far his assessment of the situation accorded with his experience, and was perfectly accurate. He had seen and spoken to ex-peasants in service with the rich, or in the dosshouses of Moscow; and he had had ample opportunity of observing them in their original surroundings. He could hardly have gone wrong. As soon, however, as his economic thought began to extend beyond what he had actually seen and heard, his sympathy for the victims of spoliation led him on to construct a curiously elaborate economic model, marred by inconsistent analysis, which will not stand up to critical examination for a minute.

The classical economists, of whom the most prominent was Adam Smith,[4] had identified three factors in the production of wealth, namely land, or the sum total of resources available in nature; labour, or all productive human effort, which, before it can be exerted, requires land, in the form of a plot to cultivate, raw materials, or a place to work; and capital, which is wealth set aside for the production of more wealth, or wealth in the process of exchange. They differed among themselves about some of the finer points; and the definitions they gave were not always mutually exclusive; but this can be taken as a rough summary of the basis on which they erected their theories. Tolstoy, however, would have nothing to do with the idea that there were only three factors of production, and proposed the additional ones of sunshine, water, air, social security, food, clothing, education and ability to speak. He could have filled a book with them, he said. Had he thought a bit more carefully, he would have realised that sunshine, water and air fall into the economic category of land; that food and clothing are wealth either in the process of exchange, when they are capital, or in the hands of the consumer, when they are wealth pure and simple; and that education, the ability to speak, and social security (meant presumably in its literal sense) are elements of labour.

When he turned from factors of production to human occupations, he showed a similar tendency to create unnecessary complications. Having made up his mind that labour was exclusively manual, he saw the peasants and factory hands as the only genuine producers. The non-producers he listed in the following order: big financiers – big industrialists – mine owners – great landowners and officials – middle-sized bankers, merchants, officials and landowners (of whom he was one) – petty traders – inn-keepers – usurers – policemen – teachers – chanters – clerks – servants – water-carriers – cabmen – pedlars.

'Big financiers' came first because, in the early 1880s, he considered, as many people still do, that money was the instrument of the enslavement of the majority to a minority. In support of this opinion, he quoted two examples, one in general terms from ancient history, and the other more specific and modern. In ancient history, the first stage was the raid, a single operation conducted with the aim of carrying off human and material booty. The second stage was a more permanent arrangement based either on chattel slavery, or on a claim to ownership of the land, which would then be divided up for exploitation by one's followers. This involved the followers in the inconvenience of personal supervision, which would suggest the advantages of stage three, the levying of a periodic tribute. What Tolstoy failed to see during this early phase of his thinking, though no doubt his account of events is substantially correct, was that stage three was merely a more subtle way of taking advantage of land-ownership. Why bother to oversee work on the land, when all you need to do is exact the rent?

Tolstoy's hazy understanding of political economy and its terminology is further illustrated by the following quotation from *Anna Karenina,* published three years before the move to Moscow:

> He [i.e. Levin, alias Tolstoy] saw that Metrov, like all the rest, in spite of his article refuting the teachings of the economists, still looked at the position of the Russian peasant merely from the standpoint of capital, wages and rent [he meant either *interest, wages* and *rent* or capital, *labour and land*]. *Though he would indeed have been obliged to admit that in the eastern, and by far the larger, part of Russia there was no such thing as rent, that for nine-tenths of Russia's eighty millions wages meant no more than a bare subsistence,* and that capital did not exist except in the form of the most primitive tools, yet he regarded every labourer from that one point of view – though in many points he disagreed with the economists and had his own theory of pay, which he expounded to Levin.[5]

If agricultural capital in Russia then consisted only 'of the most primitive tools', the conclusion must be that interest, or the return on capital, may be taken to be negligible, and that the total produce therefore fell to be divided into only two parts, wages and rent. It is frankly incredible that, in these circumstances, most of Russia should yield but a bare subsistence to the labourer as wages, and nothing at all to the landowner.

Make of all this what one will, in the ancient situation described by Tolstoy, the terms 'tribute' and 'rent' denote the same phenomenon. In other words, it is ownership of the land by the minority, and not the payment of money, that accounts for the subjection of the majority. At this time he had succeeded neither in proving his case nor in evolving on his own a coherent economic philosophy.

His second example was the occupation of the Fiji Islands by the Americans, who, he relates, seized much of the best land for cotton and coffee plantations, hired natives to work them, and treated them as slaves. So far, Tolstoy's argument cannot be faulted: seizure of the best land would have deprived many natives of their source of livelihood, and compelled them to work for the Americans on terms fixed from unequal bargaining positions. Conflicts with the natives then gave the Americans an excuse, Tolstoy went on, to demand $45,000 in compensation. This is his third stage, that of exacting tribute. When the natives failed to pay the money – for the simple reason that they had none – the Americans seized more land, and raised their demand to $90,000. In order to escape from this predicament, the nominal rulers of Fiji, in 1868, signed an agreement with an Australian trading company, whereby the company paid off the Fijians' debt in return for 200,000 more acres of their best land, with freedom from all taxes, and the exclusive right to establish banks and issue bank-notes.

This left the local rulers with no alternative for their own source of revenue but a poll tax, to raise which the natives had to resort in large numbers to the Americans and Australians for employment and wages in cash. Tolstoy's contention here was that the exaction of sums of money in fact replaced the confiscation of the land as a means of enslavement. His analysis was fallacious. It was because the land stayed confiscated that the natives were forced into the state of hired labour. The intruders' strength rested simply and solely on their possession of the land. The 'big financiers', the 'middle-sized bankers' and the 'usurers', unless they happen also to be landowners, may accordingly be deleted from Tolstoy's list of non-producers who enslave the producers. The latter have already been enslaved by the 'great landowners', the 'mine owners' and the 'middle-sized landowners'.

The same may be said of the 'great industrialists'; for, when men are assembled in large numbers for the production of an article, it is necessary for some of them to supervise the activities of the others, and provide the capital. They also have to undertake such responsibilities as estimating the demand for their products, and deciding on prices that will be competitive and also represent an adequate return on their outlay.

To continue with the list, it is hard to agree that 'merchants', 'petty traders' [including 'inn-keepers' and 'pedlars'] are unproductive. Trade, on a large or small scale, has been attested from the earliest times, and, under conditions in which land is available on equal terms to all, should be to the advantage of all participants. Based on occupational specialisation, it should ensure that peoples and individuals produce the goods and services for which their abilities best suit them, and receive in return for their surplus such goods and services as others are better able to provide. By such means, the aggregate wealth of the world is increased. How it is distributed depends to a considerable degree on the allocation of land rights.

Given Tolstoy's attitude to the State, it is surprising that he did not classify officials and policemen as counter – rather than non-productive; but at least there is no need for further discussion of this subject. It is also surprising to see 'teachers' on the list. Did he not think, while he was running his schools for peasants' children, that he was helping them to grow up to be more intelligent and efficient peasants, and therefore more productive? The remainder, as he probably realised, were innocent victims of the social system, exploited not exploiting.

This then was the Russian economic problem as Tolstoy saw it in the first half of the 1880s. The only genuine producers were those, such as peasants and factory workers, who worked with their hands; and all other categories of occupation came under the heading of 'exploiters'. It would be unrealistic to expect these opinions to remain unamended for the last thirty years of his life – he was far too volatile for that, and there was room for improvement – but there is no reason to doubt the sincerity with which he held them, remarkable enough in a man of his wealth and antecedents, or to question the genuineness of his search for the 'green stick' and its secret.

Chapter 10
Quest for the 'green stick'

I will arise and go now, and go to Innisfree,
And a small cabin build there, of clay and wattles made;
Nine bean rows will I have there, a hive for the honey-bee,
And live alone in the bee-loud glade.
William Butler Yeats.

THERE may be much to cavil at in Tolstoy's analysis, during the years 1881 to 1886, of the reason for the maldistribution of wealth; but there had been a time, on his return from the Crimean War (1854-56), when he had seen the problem in much simpler terms. It is quite understandable that he should have done so; for all his economic experience until then had been of his own extravagant consumption of an unearned rental income, and of his observations of the ill-rewarded agricultural labour of the serfs on his estate. The marvel is not only that he troubled himself to think at all about economic injustice from which he derived material benefit, but also that he tried to take action to improve the serfs' condition at his own expense.

Agriculture is the primary settled industry of mankind, and has been carried on since the 7th millennium B.C. It would therefore be hard to find anybody, except perhaps a habitual and incurious town-dweller, to deny that agricultural wealth, in the form of grain, meat, milk and its derivatives, is the result of labour applied to land. It should furthermore be obvious to any thinking person that the first claim to this wealth is that of the people who have supplied the labour to produce it, and that the second claim is that of those who, in exchange for a share of the labourers' produce, furnish them with a share of their own. Any single third party claim to a share, and a major one at that, on the pretext of having supplied the land, which has been in existence for billions of years, would be met with ribald laughter if it had not already been established since beyond living memory. That there might, in some circumstances, be a collective claim to such a share was an idea that had not yet been suggested to Tolstoy.

When he arrived back at Yasnaya Polyana in May 1856, he had already made up his mind to a compromise between his feelings of guilt as a battener on the labours of others, and the practical consideration of how he was going to provide for himself, to say nothing of repaying the mortgage he had incurred to settle his gambling debts.

Beyond all doubt, the serfs would have to be freed – this had already been mooted as a political question – but Tolstoy was clear-sighted and generous enough, unlike the legislators of the U.S.A. after 1865, to see that formal freedom without land rights would be tantamount to no freedom at all. What he therefore proposed to his serfs was immediate freedom and thirty years as his tenants, after which the land would belong to them outright.

To his surprise, they demurred. They were astute enough to realise that formal freedom was soon to be granted to them anyway by the State, but innocent enough to assume that Tolstoy's estate would immediately become *de jure* what they had always considered it to be *de facto,* namely theirs. When Tolstoy realised this, he found it very alarming. If these ideas are held generally, he thought, then one day the serfs will rise up in arms against their masters. In a moment of panic, he wrote as follows to a minister called Bludov:

... I confess I have never understood why it could not be established that the land belongs to the landlords, and the peasants be freed without giving them the land. ... Freeing them with the land is not, in my opinion, a solution. Who is to answer these questions that are essential to a solution of the overall problem, namely: how much land shall go to each, or what share of the estate; how is the landlord to receive compensation; over what period of time; who is to pay the compensation? ....[1]

He need not have worried, even momentarily. According to the imperial manifesto of 1861, the serfs were not to be freed immediately, but over a transitional period of two years, during which they were to continue to obey their owner, but the owner was not to dispose of them or their children in any way. Those, such as domestic workers, who were not subject to the *adscriptio glebae* (Ch.5) would not be entitled to receive any land, but might seek employment elsewhere. Many would do so, as Tolstoy was to observe, twenty years later, in the mansions and factories of the towns. For those who were so subject, the official conditions were less generous than the ones they could have secured from Tolstoy; but, as we have seen (Ch.6), he did his best for a while as an 'arbiter of the peace' to see that they were not even less favourable to the peasants in practice than they were in theory. For a more satisfactory 'solution of the overall problem', and a more comprehensive answer to the questions he had put to Bludov, he was to wait another twenty-seven or so years; and then they were to be not at all what he had expected, and a cause of both personal heart-searching and domestic strife.

When the dawn of enlightenment came, some time between 1883 and 1886, with his first taste of the economic philosophy of Henry George,[2] he was caught in two minds, and, for the time being, his personal view of the secret of the green stick that was to do away with human ills was the one that was uppermost. If the social problems he had observed were caused by the activities of financiers, industrialists, mine owners, officials, traders, policemen, teachers, clerks, servants and cabmen, then the new society of which he would be the prophet would be one in which these occupations no longer existed:

Just what to do? – everyone asks, and I, too, asked it as long as, under the influence of a high opinion of my vocation, I did not see that my first and unquestionable business was to procure my own food, clothing, heating, and dwelling, and in doing this to serve others, because since the beginning of the world that has been the first and surest obligation of every man.[3]

He would 'serve others' in this way, he thought, because, by providing for his own basic needs, he would no longer be requisitioning their labour, and consequently exploiting them. Self-sufficiency was to be his first aim in life; and this was the beginning of determined efforts to hold his own with peasants in the performance of field-work, and to make his own footwear, not particularly well if his friends are to be believed.

It was not only the matter of self-sufficiency that preyed on Tolstoy's mind, but the very concept of property. Where we have hitherto come across it, in association with his well-grounded ideas on the origin of wars, it has had a clear reference to land; but personal property also, as the following extract clearly shows, caused him some twinges of conscience:

> We know, or if we do not know it is easy to perceive, that property is clearly a means of appropriating other men's work. And the work of others can certainly not be my own. It has even nothing in common with the conception of property (that which is one's own) – a conception which is very exact and definite. Man always has called, and always will call, 'his own' that which is subject to his will and attached to his consciousness, namely, his own body. As soon as a man calls something his 'property' that is not his own body but something that he wishes to make subject to his will as his body is – he makes a mistake, acquires for himself disillusionment and suffering, and finds himself obliged to cause others to suffer.[4]

'Property' is therefore, in his view, not only the thing appropriated, but also the means of appropriating. This poses a dilemma that can be satisfactorily resolved only when the term itself has been resolved into its component elements of 'land' and 'wealth'.

So, despite his normally successful efforts to be a 'free-thinker', Tolstoy had not yet learned to follow a line of economic reasoning to its logical end, but had allowed his enthusiasm to carry him somewhat beyond it. What he was advocating, whether he knew it or not, was a return to a much earlier stage of human development. As Henry George was later to put it:

In the primitive stage of human life the readiest way of satisfying desires is by adapting to human use what is found in existence. In a later and more settled stage it is discovered that certain desires can be more easily and more fully satisfied by utilising the principle of growth and reproduction, as by cultivating vegetables and breeding animals. And in a still later period of development, it becomes obvious that certain desires can be better and more easily satisfied by exchange, which brings out the principle of co-operation more fully and powerfully than could obtain among unexchanging economic units.[5]

An outstanding example of this principle of cooperation by exchange was flourishing in the Russia of Tolstoy's own time, and in a way that could not possibly justify the slur of exploitation, at least before the 'semi-factories' arose. Here is a contemporary account of it by Prince P.A. Kropotkin and J.T. Bealby.

The peculiar feature of Russian industry is the development out of the domestic petty handicrafts of central Russia of a semi-factory on a large scale. Owing to the forced abstention from agricultural labour in the winter months the peasants of central Russia, more especially those of the governments (i.e. administrative areas) of Moscow, Vladimir, Yaroslavl, Kostroma, Tver, Smolensk and Ryazañ, have for centuries carried on a variety of domestic handicrafts during the period of compulsory leisure. The usual practice was for the whole of the people in one village to devote themselves to one special occupation. Thus, while one village would produce nothing but felt shoes, another would carve sacred images *(ikons),* and a third spin flax only, a fourth make wooden spoons, a fifth nails, a sixth iron chains, and so on. ...
... A good deal of the internal trade is carried on by travelling merchants.[6]

In preaching self-sufficiency, despite all such activities, Tolstoy was reaching back to Henry George's stage two, but at the same time, inconsistently no doubt, being unable to ignore the welfare of his wife and children, he retained his rents, the reward, as he himself had admitted, of the non-producer.

As for his 'high opinion of his vocation', presumably as the author of *War and Peace* and *Anna Karenina,* each of which has been acclaimed as the finest novel in the world, and perhaps also as the seeker of the green stick, Tolstoy was really being too modest. Would he not have recognised himself, on both counts, in the following definition by Henry George?

He who by any exertion of mind or body adds to the aggregate of enjoyable wealth, increases the sum of human knowledge or gives to human life higher elevation or greater fulness – he is, in the large meaning of the words, a 'producer', a 'working-man', a 'labourer', and is honestly earning honest wages. But he who without doing aught to make mankind richer, wiser, better, happier, lives on the toil of others – he, no matter by what name of honour he may be called, or how lustily the priests of Mammon may swing their censers before him, is in the last analysis but a beggarman or a thief.[7]

Tolstoy could then with reason have gone on being proud of his achievements as a writer, while being ashamed of his rôle as an absorber of rent; but his subsequent actions in renouncing royalties on his writings, and attempting to evade the guilt of rent-collection by making his land over to his family, are signs of continuing failure to recognise the royalties as 'honest wages', as defined by Henry George, and the rents as the proceeds of robbery, from the responsibility for which he could not absolve himself by passing it on.

There remains his pride in his prowess as a farm-labourer and boot-maker, by which he imagined he was easing the burden on the people who were accustomed to doing these jobs for a livelihood. He had made up his mind, in fact, that there was something wrong with the division of labour, while we, on the other hand, have shown some reason for its being a potent influence for human progress. It is interesting to see how Matthew Arnold also had made up his mind on this subject, somewhat differently but with an equal lack of accurate analytical thought:

... I do not know how it is in Russia, but in an English village the determination of 'our circle' to earn their bread by the work of their hands would produce only dismay, not fraternal joy, amongst that 'majority' who are so earning it already. 'There are plenty of us to compete as things stand', the gardeners, carpenters, and smiths would say; 'pray stick to your articles, your poetry, and nonsense; in manual labour you will interfere with us, and be taking the bread out of our mouths'.[8]

It is to be feared that Arnold, for all his self-imposed obligation[9] of spreading 'sweetness and light' and making 'the will of God prevail' among the 'Barbarians' [the English landed gentry], the 'Philistines' [the English middle class] and the 'Populace', and his readiness, with Tolstoy, to strip the accretions of the later Church from the pure doctrines and example of Christ, was a high Tory in his economics. He took it for granted that there must be competition for work among those people who regard literature as 'nonsense', and that any attempt to join them in the struggle is decidedly unkind.

Henry George maintained, on the contrary, that, in an undistorted economy, which his remedy of the single tax would bring about, any competition that existed would be among prospective employers of labour. It is time, therefore, to note the first impression that he made on the turmoil of Tolstoy's economic ideas between 1883 and 1886:

Where violence is legalized, there slavery exists. ...

A striking illustration of the truth of this conclusion is supplied by Henry George's project for nationalizing the land. George proposes to recognize all land as belonging to the State, and therefore to replace all taxes, both direct and indirect, by a ground rent. That is to say, every one making use of land should pay to the State the rental-value of such land.

What would result? Agricultural slavery would be abolished within the bounds of the State, that is, the land would belong to the State: England would have its own, America its own, and the slave-dues a man had to pay would be determined by the amount of land he used.

Perhaps the position of some of the workers (agrarian) would be improved, but as long as the forcible collection of a rent tax remained – there would be slavery. An agriculturalist unable after a failure of crops to pay the rent forcibly demanded of him, to retain his land and not lose everything would have to go into bondage to a man who had money.[10]

There are clear indications here – 'the amount of land he used', 'the workers (agrarian)' – that Tolstoy had not yet understood George, and was in a suitable frame of mind anyway to reject his ideas. We must be fair to him though, and emphasise that the first of George's books that be read was not *Progress and Poverty* (1879), in which George's economic philosophy is set forth with patient and exhaustive logic, but *Social Problems* (1883), the first thirteen chapters of which had started life as articles in *Frank Leslie's Illustrated Newspaper,* and which dwelt on the problems rather than on economic theory. George's eloquent descriptions of poverty in New York stand comparison with Tolstoy's of poverty in Moscow; and it was probably these that first attracted him.

What would on the contrary have repelled him initially was George's simple explanation of poverty as opposed to his own complicated one, and the fact that the single tax, so far as it was possible to foresee, required state action. The State, he claimed with justification, is based on violence, and maintains itself by violence. Therefore, he reasoned with rather less justification, the levying of the single tax would be an act of violence. George, however, did not believe in violence any more than Tolstoy did; so the next step must be to examine George's philosophy more carefully, and to see how Tolstoy in the end became won over to it.

Chapter 11
The Single Tax

*Both ground-rents and the ordinary rent of land are a
species of revenue which the owner, in many cases, enjoys
without any care or attention of his own. Though a part of
this revenue should be taken from him in order to defray
the expences of the state, no discouragement will thereby
be given to any sort of industry. The annual produce of the
land and labour of the society, the real wealth and revenue
of the great body of the people, might be the same after
such a tax as before. Ground-rents, and the ordinary rent
of land, are, therefore, perhaps, the species of revenue
which can best bear to have a peculiar tax imposed upon
them.*
Adam Smith.

W HEN one is studying the life of a man such as Tolstoy,
with unconventional ideas to which, in his own writings,
he gives the forceful and dramatic expression suited to a wide
audience, it is sometimes instructive to turn to those of an
intimate friend, in order to catch the tone of the great man's
musings during his more relaxed moments. Here is such a
moment, as recorded by Aylmer Maude, from a time when
Tolstoy had come to a better understanding of Henry George's
philosophy:

Speaking of the same subject [i.e. of the progress made in the
dissemination of this philosophy], Tolstoy remarked that some
men are born with the qualities and the *limitations* that enable
them to concentrate their powers on some one subject that needs
attention, and to see all that relates to it without seeing anything
that would turn their energies in other directions. So we get a

80

Cobden to abolish corn-laws, and a Henry George to elucidate the
land question. God needs such labourers as much as he does men
of a wider sweep of perception.[1]

It will probably now never be known whether this particular
conversation was being conducted in Russian or in English; for
each had a more than adequate knowledge of the other's
language. In either case, Tolstoy's attitude to manual work
makes it highly unlikely that the word 'labourers' or its Russian
equivalent was intended to convey any pejorative meaning –
rather the contrary. The only question is: was Tolstoy – who
evidently regarded himself as having a 'wider sweep of
perception' than either Cobden or George – correct in this
view in so far as George was concerned, or was the difference
between them one of emphasis only?

Certainly Tolstoy, whether he was writing about a more
rational Christianity, or about the criminality of the State,
social evils in general, land reform, vegetarianism, temperance
or any other subject near to his heart, turned his full attention
on it, like a spotlight, so that a casual reader might suppose it to
be the only subject about which he had deep feelings. George,
on the contrary, took involuntary poverty as his starting point.
Tracing its origin solely to the unequal distribution of rights to
land, he, it should not be forgotten, also saw it as being in its
turn the origin of many more of the ills that afflict humanity,
which caused him no less concern. As a result, his remedy,
which he not only wrote down but toured the world to talk
about, was distinguished by the clinical precision of a tablet of
glyceryl trinitrate, which forestalls a heart attack by dilating the
cardiac arteries, but does not directly affect any other bodily
organ whatsoever.

Unlike Tolstoy, the landed aristocrat, George was a man of
the people, and had personal experience of poverty. He was
born in Philadelphia in 1839, eleven years later than Tolstoy,
into a middle class family of mixed English, Scottish and Welsh
ancestry. His father began and ended as a Customs House clerk,
with a seventeen year interval as a publisher of religious books.
Henry, by contrast, went to sea at the age of sixteen as a

foremast boy on an old East Indiaman, bound for Melbourne and Calcutta by way of the Cape of Good Hope. It was during the last stages of the journey to Calcutta, up the Hooghly branch of the Ganges, that, as his son Henry George, Jr., records, the eventual pattern of his life was set:

> Then came the first impressions of the country – impressions that always afterward remained vivid and helped before long to direct thought to social questions; that changed the fancied India – the place of dreamy luxury, of soft and sensuous life – into the real India, with its extremes of light and shadow, of poverty and riches, of degradation and splendour; where the few have so much, the many so little; where jewels blaze in the trappings of elephants, but where, as he has since said in talking with his son Richard, 'the very carrion birds are more sacred than human life!'[2]

In June 1856, the old sailing-ship completed her return voyage, and dropped anchor in New York Bay.

From the autumn of 1856 to December 1857, George worked for a large printing firm in Philadelphia, and not only learned the trade of type-setting, which was later to stand him in good stead, but got into the habit of absorbing, considering and discussing pieces of information of all kinds. One such item, brought to his attention by a senior colleague, was the fact that, while in old countries wages are low, in new countries they are always high. This seeming paradox haunted him for a long time, until the answer to it gave him the clue he needed for his great discovery.

After this, and another brief spell as a seaman on a coastal trader, he received an appointment as storekeeper on board a ship destined for service as a lighthouse tender on the west coast. He arrived in San Francisco in May 1858, in time to join the rush of 50,000 people to the mouth of the Frazer River, where large quantities of gold were said to have been discovered. As he was later to write:

> It was the discovery of placer mines in unappropriated land to which labour was free that raised the wages of cooks in San Francisco restaurants to $500 a month, and left ships to rot in the

harbour without officers or crew until their owners would consent to pay rates that in any other part of the globe seemed fabulous. Had these mines been on appropriated land, or had they been immediately monopolised so that rent could have arisen, it would have been land values that would have leaped upward, not wages.[3]

The reports of gold turned out to have been exaggerated; but their observed effects provided yet more food for thought for the budding political economist.

On his return to San Francisco, in November 1858, George entered on a period of his life characterised by alternate phases of adversity and relative prosperity in the world of printing and journalism. One of his homes during this time was a room in an hotel named 'What cheer house', where a young ex-Army captain called Ulysses Simpson Grant, a future President of the United States, had stayed four years before. One of its features was a little library of several hundred well-selected books, including some on economics. In later years, George was to tell a friend that this was where he had begun his serious reading, and had in fact seen there for the first time a copy of Adam Smith's *Wealth of Nations*, though he did not remember actually reading it then.

Whatever doubts there may be about the relative weight to be attached to his personal observations and his reading – and he himself always maintained that reading came second – there is no doubt at all about the milestone in the progress of his thought represented by an article that he wrote for the *Overland Monthly* in October 1868, entitled 'What the railroad will bring us'. It referred to the transcontinental railway, then nearing completion:

The truth is, that the completion of the railroad and the consequent great increase of business and population, will not be a benefit to all of us, but only to a portion. As a general rule (liable of course to exceptions) those who have, it will make wealthier; for those *who have not,* it will make it more difficult to get. Those who have lands, mines, established businesses, special abilities of certain kinds, will become richer for it and find increased opportunities; those who have only their own labour will become poorer, and find it harder to get ahead – first because it will take more capital to buy land or to get into business; and second, because as competition reduces the wages of labour, this capital will be harder for them to obtain.[4]

He had not yet achieved the startling clarity of his later work; but he was, as it were, struggling towards the light.

The moment of illumination came when the railway had reached Sacramento, and there was a proposal to extend it to Oakland. As a result, there was a great rush to buy and to hold as much land as possible in order to benefit from the rise in its value that an increasing population would bring. One afternoon, while all this was going on, the young Henry George went for a ride. This, in his own words, is what happened to him:

> Absorbed in my own thoughts, I had driven the horse into the hills until he panted. Stopping for breath, I asked a passing teamster, for want of something better to say, what land was worth there. He pointed to some cows grazing off so far that they looked like mice and said: 'I don't know exactly, but there is a man over there who will sell some land for a thousand dollars an acre'. Like a flash it came upon me that there was the reason of advancing poverty with advancing wealth. With the growth of population, land grows in value, and the men who work it must pay more for the privilege. I turned back, amidst quiet thought, to the perception that then came to me and has been with me ever since.[5]

The clue to the problem of poverty having surfaced in a moment of inspiration, it remained for George to work his way through to a solution by means of the principles of political economy.

Tolstoy, the imaginative literary artist, had considered the traditional concept of three factors of production, namely land, labour and capital, had added some more of his own invention, and had claimed that there were enough of them to fill a book. As we have seen, he was mistaken. George, on the contrary, recognised the general correctness of the three, but refined their definitions so as to make them individually comprehensive, and mutually exclusive.

The clear definition of terms is an essential preliminary to any kind of scientific thinking. There is, for example, a proof of the irrationality of the square root of 2; but the first step towards its discovery was a clear mathematical statement of the problem itself. This is that the square root of 2 cannot be expressed by any fraction a/b, where 'a' and 'b' are integers with no common factor; for, if they had one, it could be eliminated. The idea having been clarified, the rest is simple. So it is with the science of political economy. Here are its definitions, when they had been given their final polish by Henry George:

Land: All the material universe outside of man and his products.

Labour: All human exertion, mental or physical, directed towards the production of wealth.

Wealth: Any material thing produced by human labour – using land both as a source of raw materials and as a location for work – so as to fit the raw materials for the satisfaction of human needs and desires.

Capital: Both wealth used in the production of more wealth and wealth in the course of production or exchange.

Rent: The share of wealth that accrues to the owners of land by virtue of their ownership.

Wages: The share of wealth that is the return for labour.

Interest: The share of wealth that is the return for the use of capital in production.

Tolstoy's word 'property', about which he drew such far-reaching conclusions, contains suggestions of both 'land' and 'wealth', and has therefore no part in this scheme of things.

So much for the terminology. The problem itself, why poverty persists in the midst of advancing wealth, needed to be redefined before it could be treated in a scientific way; and this is how George did it:

> Why, in spite of increase in productive power, do wages tend to a minimum which will give but a bare living?[6]

In his *Progress and Poverty,* George noted the work of the French Physiocrats, who, failing to recognise the significance of land for industry and commerce, proposed merely a single tax on the value of agricultural and mining land. He denied, however, with some satisfaction at having reached his own more comprehensive conclusion by way of a sounder line of reasoning, that his work owed anything to theirs. In his own words:

> Without knowing anything of Quesnay or his doctrines, I have reached the same practical conclusion by a route which cannot be disputed and have based it on grounds which cannot be questioned by the accepted political economy.[7]

He freely admitted, on the other hand, his debt to David Ricardo and his law of rent. This law, a central one to all honest economic thinking, runs as follows:

> *The rent of land is determined by the excess of its produce over that which the same application can secure from the least productive land in use.*[8]

This 'least productive land in use' is often referred to as the 'margin of production'. So expressed, the law of rent can present difficulties even to intelligent and enquiring minds, especially those accustomed to thinking in terms of visual images rather than of abstractions. 'Where', one hears it asked, 'is this marginal land? Could you show me some?' A way round this difficulty, a severe one where urban land is concerned, is to consider primarily, not the land, but the processes of production and exchange, and to put the law in this way:

Ricardo demonstrated that the rent of land is a specific, not an arbitrary, quantity, and represents a return to ownership over and above the return which is sufficient to induce use.[9]

We can now see the distribution of wealth, as George himself did, in terms of equations:

Wealth = Rent + Wages + Interest

or, to express the law of rent algebraically:

Rent = Wealth − (Wages + Interest)

It is now easy to understand George's comments on the situation in San Francisco at the time of the Frazer River gold rush. So long as the means existed, or even while people *thought* they existed, for earning a living elsewhere on their own account, then the restaurant owners in San Francisco, and the owners of the ships in the harbour, would not get away with offering the cooks and sailors less in wages than they thought they were going to earn for themselves. The principle is of general application. While unoccupied land still exists, the general level of wages will not sink below what those who go to occupy it consider, on the basis of the qualities of similar land, that they are going to earn.

But what happens when all land is occupied? The majority of people are obliged to look for employment in the enterprises of others. In these circumstances, basic wages will sink to the lowest level that seekers for work are willing to accept. This will vary according to the power of trade unions at the particular time and place, and to the level of public provision for the poor. Where there is no such provision and no such trade union power, basic wages will be such as barely to keep the worker alive; for nobody could work for less. If there is a dole, by whatever comforting euphemism it is known, basic wages will not be lower than the dole; for why work for less than what you can get without working? Here is the answer to the question asked by the old printer in Philadelphia: why wages are low in old countries, but high in new.

It follows naturally from these considerations that any improvements on the productive side, whether resulting from new inventions, more effective education, increasing specialisation, or any other cause whatsoever, will do nothing to improve the bargaining position of those who labour but possess no land; so their wages *will* not increase as a result of such phenomena. What will increase is rent, and in consequence the value of land. To make matters worse, the holders of the land come to take production improvements for granted, and to demand rents in excess of what current methods can stand. Hence the familiar periodic booms and slumps, or business cycles, which defy analysis by methods that take no account of rising and falling land values, but were easily accounted for by Henry George.

More damaging still, in the absence of any charge associated with the ownership of land, is the opportunity offered to the cunning and unscrupulous to hold quantities of it far in excess of their capacity for using it, but merely as an investment for the future. Then, when growing needs increase the demand for it, and therefore its value, it is possible to accumulate vast fortunes merely by staying alive for long enough. Such activity, or lack of it, had been obvious and notorious in the United States from its very beginnings. It still takes place both there and in older countries, such as Britain, but is rather less obvious. A more noticeable phenomenon in Britain is the owning of thousands of acres of both urban and rural land, the enjoyment of unearned income from high urban rents and rural ones inflated by agricultural subsidies, and the use for purposes of 'sport' of parts of the country, such as the highlands of Scotland, that once supported a large population. There is no need to seek further for the cause of unemployment and poverty.

The single tax, or the abolition of existing taxes on production and consumption and the collection for public revenue of something approaching the whole annual rental value of land, which value would after all not exist but for the public presence, and cannot be said to have been earned by anybody in particular, would change all this, argued George.

Alone among taxes, it could not be 'passed on'; for, by definition, rent is already at a maximum. Furthermore, by putting an end to non-productive holding, it would bring on to the market all potentially productive land commensurate with current needs, making it available on equal terms to all those with the will and ability to use it, who would in consequence be seeking employees instead of having employees seeking them. Wages would rise to their natural level of a full equivalent to value added by labour; and involuntary poverty would be at an end. Poverty, it will be remembered, or at any rate the 'unequal distribution of property', which here could include both land and wealth, was, in Tolstoy's well-considered judgment, the primary cause of war.

Chapter 12
Tolstoy on Henry George

*Each time a man stands up for an ideal, or acts to improve
the lot of others, or strikes out against injustice, he sends
forth a tiny ripple of hope ... and crossing each other from
a million different centers of energy and daring those
ripples build a current that can sweep down the mightiest
walls of oppression and resistance.*
Robert F. Kennedy.

POSSIBLY somewhere in the Tolstoy archives there exists
some clue as to when he revised his first unfavourable
opinion of the doctrines of Henry George. It may be that, when
he re-read *Social Problems,* and discovered the following
disarming statement, he realised after all that state violence
was the last thing George had in mind for the application of his
single tax:

> Social reform is not to be secured by noise and shouting; by com-
> plaints and denunciation; by the formation of parties, or the
> making of revolutions; but by the awakening of thought and the
> progress of ideas. Until there be correct thought, there cannot be
> right action; and when there is correct thought, right action *will*
> follow. Power is always in the hands of the masses of men. What
> oppresses the masses is their own ignorance, their own short-
> sighted selfishness.[1]

George did not include a working knowledge of French
among his accomplishments, and knew, for example, what he
knew of the Physiocrats of the 18th century through
commentaries written in English. It is therefore extremely
unlikely that he had the slightest inkling of the parallel

sentiments, already quoted as being familiar to Tolstoy, of the 16th century writer Etienne de la Boétie (Ch. 6). There is a strong probability that all three men were right in thinking that popular awareness of the machinery of oppression is all that is required for its removal.

What is certain about Tolstoy's change of front, easily understandable in the light of his already observed general volatility, is that, on the 24th November 1894, he wrote a letter to a certain Ernest Crosby in very different terms from those of 1886:

> If the new Tsar were to ask me what I would advise him to do, I would say to him: use your autocratic power to abolish the land property in Russia and to introduce the single tax system; and then give up your power and (give) the people a liberal constitution.[2]

His new opinion of the single tax was evidently so high that he was ready to condone just one more act of violence in order to see it put into operation. What more could an advocate of non-violence say?

On the 9th August of the same year, he had already written in his private diary:

> During this time MacGahan [the Russian-born widow of an American journalist] and her son visited me and brought some books from Henry George. Read *A perplexed philosopher* again. Excellent. Became very vividly aware again of the sin of owning land. It's astonishing that people don't see it. How necessary to write a book about this – to write a new *Uncle Tom's Cabin*. Yesterday I received an article from Sergeyev and an article from *Gegen den Strom*. How much truth is spoken on all sides, and how little of it is heard by people. Something else is needed.[3]

A Perplexed Philosopher (1892)[4] was Henry George's reaction to Herbert Spencer's abandonment of a doctrine, defined in his *Social Statics* (1850), whereby ownership of land would be resumed by the State, which would then let it out in parcels to all desiring to become state tenants. Whereas, however, Spencer's plan would require the setting up of a special department of the bureaucracy, George's would merely require existing departments for valuation and revenue raising to demand the bulk of the rent, leaving just enough of it to those holding land beyond their own requirements to make it worth their while to act as the State's agents for collection.[5] *A Perplexed Philosopher* is an exemplary polemic, increasing gradually in heat, against an undoubted defection from the cause of natural justice.

In 1897, Tolstoy was to write to T.M. Bondarev:

When all the land in the country has been valued in this way, Henry George proposes that a law should be made by which, after a certain date in a certain year, the land should no longer belong to any one individual, but to the whole nation – the whole people; and that everyone holding land should therefore pay to the nation (that is, to the whole people) the yearly value at which it has been assessed. This payment should be used to meet all public or national expenses, and should replace all other rates, taxes, or customs dues.

The result of this would be that a landed proprietor who now holds, say, 2,000 desyatins, might continue to hold them if he liked, but he would have to pay to the treasury – here in the Tula Government for instance (as his holding would include both meadow-land and homestead) – 12,000 or 15,000 rubles a year; and, as no large landowners could stand such a payment, they would all abandon their land. But it would mean that a Tula peasant in the same district would pay a couple of rubles per desyatin less than he pays now, and could have plenty of available land near by which he could take up at 5 or 6 rubles per desyatin. Besides this, he would have no other rates or taxes to pay, and would be able to buy all the things he requires, foreign or Russian, free of duty. In towns, the owners of houses and factories might continue to own them, but would have to pay to the public treasury the amount of the assessment on their land.

The advantages of such an arrangement would be:

1. That no one would be unable to get land for use.

2. That there would be no idle people owning land and making others work for them in return for permission to use that land.

3. That the land would be in the possession of those who use it, and not of those who do not use it.

4. That as the land would be available for people who wished to work on it, they would cease to enslave themselves as hands in factories and workshops, or as servants in towns, and would settle in the country districts.

5. That there would be no more inspectors and collectors of taxes in mills, factories, refineries, and workshops, but there would only be collectors of the tax on land, which cannot be stolen, and from which a tax can be most easily collected.

6 . (and most important). That the non-workers would be saved from the sin of exploiting other people's labour (in doing which they are often not the guilty parties, for they have from childhood been educated in idleness and do not know how to work), and from the still greater sin of all kinds of shuffling and lying to justify themselves in committing that sin; and the workers would be saved from the temptation and sin of envying, condemning, and being exasperated with the non-workers, so that one cause of separation among men would be destroyed.[6]

Some of this is not quite according to Henry George, who proposed no change to titles of ownership, let alone a specified date for it. Nor is there any reason to believe that he expected 'all' holders of titles to large estates to 'abandon their land'. Indeed, as we have seen, he expected them to stay to act as revenue-collectors, even if they did not strictly speaking use the land themselves. They would, of course, be anxious to dispose of land not currently in productive use and for which they could find no tenants. Despite these inaccuracies of detail, Tolstoy has here produced an excellent summary of the advantages of the single tax; and his passionate use, in the last paragraph, of the language of religion provided precisely the emphasis needed to carry conviction with a devout reader.

In 1899, there came to fruition a plan, first hinted at in the diary entry for the 9th August 1894, and expanded in the one for the 26th May 1895, where he wrote: 'Nekhlyudov must be a follower of Henry George, and must bring this in ... ',[7] to write a book about the 'sin of owning land'. This was the novel *Resurrection*,[8] usually discussed as the story of the hero's atonement for his casual seduction of a girl, which led in the end to her being sentenced to exile for a murder she did not commit. There is what looks like a conspiracy to play down the fact that it is equally the story of how Nekhlyudov did what Tolstoy would dearly have loved to do, namely apply Henry George's principle to his own estates by devoting their rents to the peasants' welfare. In this instance, Tolstoy's conscience pulled him in two different directions. On the one hand, he was deeply committed to opposing the unconditional private ownership of land. On the other, his loyalty to his family precluded him from forcing them to live in accordance with his personal principles. Another reason for paying insufficient attention to the social criticisms in *Resurrection* is that among them are also attacks on the Orthodox Church, the legal system, and, in general, rule by violence in the interests of a minority of the population. It is, in fact, a handbook in fictional form of Tolstoy's philosophy.

It would come as something of a shock after all this, to a student unaware of Tolstoy's tendency to change his mind on important subjects, to learn that, on one occasion subsequently, in 1900, he gave way to his misgivings about the force that he thought would be necessary to put the single tax into operation:

> Those who, like Henry George and his partisans, would abolish the laws making private property of land, propose new laws imposing an obligatory rent on the land. And this obligatory land rent will necessarily create a new form of slavery; because a man compelled to pay rent or single-tax may, at any failure of the crops or other misfortune, have to borrow money from a man who has some to lend, and he will again lapse into slavery.[9]

Lest people should think that they must have misunderstood this statement, he states quite clearly in the preface to the essay:

> But, as I think that during these fifteen years I have reflected on the questions discussed in 'What must we do then?' more quietly

and minutely, in relation to the teachings at present existing and diffused among us, I now offer the reader new considerations leading to the same replies as before.[10]

What he seems here to fail to understand is that there is no question of 'imposing an obligatory rent on the land'. It exists already, by virtue of Ricardo's law (Ch.11), in the shape of the differential between the annual value of any given piece of land and that of a piece of the least productive land in use, whose economic value is nil. All that remains to be decided is whether this value belongs to some individual or to the general public. What to do in the event of a 'failure of the crops or other misfortune' is a problem that arises for tenant farmers whichever way the decision goes; but such a failure would, in any case, bring rents down.

Whatever it was that was on his mind to cause this reversion had evidently ceased to trouble him by 1902; for it was in the January of that year that he finally carried out the project mentioned in the letter of 1894 to Ernest Crosby, namely that of writing to the Tsar Nicholas II on the subject of land reform and its crucial importance if the social stresses of the time were to be peacefully relieved (see Appendix 1). In order to make sure that the Tsar received it, he sent it in the first instance to another member of the royal family, the Grand Duke Nikolay Mikhaylovich, who had taken the initiative in making Tolstoy's acquaintance in the Crimea the year before.

It would appear that neither the Tsar nor the Grand Duke was in favour of Tolstoy's proposal; for, in the Spring of the same year, he wrote a second letter to the Grand Duke (see Appendix 2), embodying a far superior definition of the single tax principle to the ones already quoted:

The essence of the project surely is that land rent, i.e. the excess value of land as compared with land of the lowest yield, and depending not on man's labour but on nature or the whereabouts of the land, is used for taxes, i.e. for common needs; i.e. the common revenue is used for the common cause. The only effect of this project is that if you own a certain amount of land in

Borzhomi and I in the Tula province, *nobody takes that land away from me,* and I am only obliged to pay a rent for it which is always lower than its yield.[11]

It will be noticed that he has by now both grasped the significance of Ricardo's law and shed the illusion that George's plan involved a mass hand-over of land to the State.

From the rest of the letter, it is evident that the Grand Duke had pleaded that a different Tsar and different ministers would be needed to do what Tolstoy wished, and that therefore administrative reforms would have to have priority. Tolstoy would have none of this, pointing out that such reforms would do nothing but support an obsolete autocracy that existed to further no high ideal, but only to maintain its own power. He was right (Ch.5). The concept of Russia as a private estate owned by its princes and nobles dated from the earliest legendary beginnings, and that of the Tsar as the Lord's Anointed from the coronation of Ivan the Terrible in 1547. Neither concept had the slightest relevance to the emerging industrial Russia of the nineteenth century.

There is one point that we need to be very clear about before going any further. We know from benefit of hindsight that, since the police raid on Yasnaya Polyana of 1862, Tolstoy suffered no practical molestation at the hands of authority; but, so far as he himself knew, he was liable at any time to be marched off to imprisonment or even death. In these circumstances, his persistent, public and vociferous advocacy of causes that he knew to be inimical to the short-term interest of the rulers of the Russian Empire called for courage of the very highest order. Scruples about compelling his family to toe the line may have led to some discrepancy between his public attitudes and private actions; but he never ceased to proclaim his faith in anarchism, rational Christianity and Georgist economics – when once he had been fully convinced of them – regardless of the risk of the most serious consequences.

Three years later, on the 21st April 1905, he wrote in his diary: 'I've begun to write *Defenders of the people.* It's not bad. And *Henry George.*[12] The latter work began as an article about Henry

George, sent in the first instance to *The Times,* but became expanded into *A Great Iniquity*. It is an eloquent denunciation of private property in land, with praise of Henry George, an account of the opposition he had met with (and still does), and extensive quotations from one of his published speeches.[13] Here is Tolstoy on the subject of the methods of George's enemies:

> At Oxford when Henry George was lecturing, the students organized a hostile demonstration, and the Roman Catholic party regarded his teaching as simply sinful, immoral, dangerous, and contrary to Christ's teaching. The orthodox science of political economy rose up against Henry George's teaching in the same way. Learned professors from the height of their superiority refuted it without understanding it, chiefly because it did not recognize the fundamental principles of their pseudo-science. The Socialists were also inimical – considering the most important problem of the period to be not the land question, but the complete abolition of private property. The chief method of opposing Henry George was, however, the method always employed against irrefutable and self-evident truths. This, which is still being applied to Henry George's teaching, was that of ignoring it. This method of hushing up was practised so successfully that Labouchere, a British Member of Parliament, could say publicly and without contradiction that he 'was not such a visionary as Henry George, and did not propose to take the land from the landlords in order afterwards to rent it out again, but that he only demanded the imposition of a tax on the value of the land'. That is, while attributing to Henry George what he could not possibly have said, Labouchere corrected that imaginary fantasy by putting forward Henry George's actual proposal.[14]

Such false attributions and corrections, accurately defined and denounced by Tolstoy in 1905, still sully the writings of critics of Henry George nearly a century later.

Diary entries for the remaining years of his life indicate Tolstoy's continuing enthusiasm for the Georgist cause. Here are those from a selection published in English:

2nd April 1906. 'People talk and argue about Henry George's system. It isn't the system which is valuable (although not only do I not know a better one, but I can't imagine one), but what is valuable is the fact that the system establishes an attitude to land which is universal and the same for everybody. Let them find a better one if they can'.[15]

6th June 1906. 'A correspondent has been, and I wrote down a few things about Henry George and told him about the Duma and the repressions'.[16]

2nd September 1906. 'Then I wrote a bit about Henry George – not well'.[17]

(The editor of the collection here informs us that this entry refers to a foreword to the Russian translation of Henry George's 'Social Problems').

24th September 1906. 'I've finished all the works I've started and written a foreword to Henry George'.[18]

19th May 1909. 'Dear Nikolayev came twice. What a wonderful worker he is in the Henry George sense, and what a good person in general'.[19]

2nd June 1909. 'A telegram from Henry George's son, then someone from the *Russian Word* with the proofs of the Mechnikov article. Corrected the proofs and wrote about Henry George and sent it to the *Russian Word*. They probably won't print it'.[20]

(This article, 'Apropos of the visit of Henry George's son', was not, the editor informs us, accepted by the 'Russian Word', but appeared in the 'Russian Gazette' on the 9th June 1909).

5th June 1909. 'Did nothing today: revised *The One Commandment* and the article on George a little bit. George's son came with a photographer. A pleasant person'.[21]

20th August 1909. 'A conversation with Tenishev about the single tax. Felt peaceful and tender-hearted'.[22]

(This shows a truly Christian attitude; for, the editor tells us, Tenishev refused to raise the matter of the single tax in the Duma).

28th August 1909. 'I invited Maklakov in and spoke to him about raising the question in the Duma. He said he knew nothing about Henry George, and that the question would not only not get through, but would not even provoke discussion. He is very clever in a practical sense, but completely deaf to all questions really necessary to people – like very, very many people'.[23]

23rd October 1909. 'Went for a walk. Weak. A pain in the small of my back. Came back, didn't feel like it at first, but then wrote down my dream about Henry George. Not entirely good, but not entirely bad either'.[24]

(This piece, the editor informs us, forms the final part of the trilogy 'Three Days in the Country').

7th November 1909. 'Yesterday morning I received a wonderful letter from Polilov about Henry George and replied to him, and something else that was pleasant too – Tolstoy's pedagogics in Bulgarian'.[25]

(The editor's research has revealed that: 'P. Polilov was a pseudonym used by Tolstoy's daughter Tatyana who had written a popular account of Henry George's teaching and wanted to get her father's impartial opinion about it. Tolstoy was taken in and wrote an enthusiastic reply. Tatyana came to Yasnaya Polyana a few days later and revealed "Polilov's" identity').

Henry George had died in New York on the 28th October 1897, during the course of an election campaign in support of his candidacy for the position of Mayor; but Tolstoy had carried on the good work undeterred. He continued to keep the pressure on politicians, writing to the Prime Minister Stolypin himself in January 1908. He used his *Posrednik* ('The Interpreter') series of low-priced booklets to publicise the great American's rousing speeches; and he kept in touch with single taxers in other countries of the world. For example, in September 1908, he wrote a letter to the Australian Georgists, who had sent him their birthday greetings. It included the following:

> ... This problem, ie., the abolition of property in land, at the present time everywhere demands its solution as insistingly as half a century ago the problem of slavery demanded its solution in Russia and America.
> This problem insistingly demands its solution because the supposed right of landed property now lies at the foundation, not only of economic misery, but also of political disorder, and, above all, the depravation [sic] of the people.
> The wealthy ruling classes, foreseeing the loss of the advantages of their position inevitable with the solution of the problem, are endeavouring by various false interpretations, justifications and palliatives, with all their power, to postpone as long as possible its solution.[26]

And to the English ones in the following March:

> As in the law of non-resistance to evil by violence, i.e. the prohibition of killing under any circumstances whatever, has been elucidated the injustice and harmfulness of the justification of violence under pretext of defence and common good, so also in Henry George's teaching on the equal rights of all to the land, has been elucidated the injustice and harmfulness of the justification of robbery and theft under the pretext of either the exclusive right of some people to the land, or the depriving of those who labour of the produce of their labour in order to use it for social needs.[27]

It was only a year later, in the October of 1910 (Ch.1), that he occupied the time during his last railway journey by talking to his fellow-passengers about those matters that were uppermost in his mind, and especially about Henry George and the single tax.

Crowds gathered at his funeral on the 9th November; and a peasant woman was heard to say to her son:

Remember him – he lived for us.

Chapter 13
Were they socialists?

*Socialism is workable only in heaven where it isn't needed,
and in hell where they've got it.*
Cecil Palmer.

L EO TOLSTOY and Henry George were in perfect accord
about the first step to be taken if economic justice is to be
restored to the world; and, after George's untimely death in
1897, we have seen Tolstoy in touch with George's disciples in
Australia and England. In the first of these two countries, some
success was achieved, during Tolstoy's lifetime, in applying the
principle of land value taxation in a limited measure to the
raising of both national and local revenue. In England,
however, where many Liberal M.P.s were strongly in favour
of it, an untrustworthy Cabinet and an obstinate opposition
delayed, modified and, on the outbreak of the First World War,
altogether prevented their proposals from being put into
practice.

It so happened that Aylmer Maude was able to give Tolstoy
an eye-witness account of events in England at the turn of the
century:

He asked me once, when I had been to England for a few weeks,
how the single-tax movement was getting on.

I said that I thought it was a small movement not making much
way.

'How is that, when the question is one of such enormous
importance?'
I said I thought that the great majority of Englishmen were too

conservative to attend to it, and the Socialists and other advanced parties had gone past Henry George and recognised interest, and private property in the means of production, as being also wrong.

'That is a pity', said Tolstoy, 'If the Conservatives are too conservative to attend to it, and the advanced parties have gone past it, who is to do this work that so urgently needs doing?'[1]

If Maude had been speaking to Tolstoy after, instead of before, 1906, the year of the Liberal landslide victory at a General Election, he might have been a little more optimistic about the prospects of the single tax in England, though ultimately his pessimism was justified. It was socialism that came out on top in the end, in a mild and temporary form in England, but in an extreme, a violent, and a somewhat longer-lasting form in Russia.

Neither Tolstoy nor George was ever to achieve political office. Tolstoy had made up his mind in 1857 never to try to do any such thing; and George had died in 1897 (Ch.12). The views of both men must therefore be judged, not on any tangible results they achieved personally in the world of politics, but on what they wrote and said. Their opinions on the single tax should already be abundantly clear; but what they thought about socialism needs also to be examined, because they were both later to be accused of being socialists.

Socialism' is a word that is apt, in general parlance, to be loosely used. It can refer to municipally-owned local enterprises for the supply of water, gas, electricity, transport and so on, which in the past have been found harmless and useful enough. At the other extreme, it can mean state ownership of every enterprise of whatever nature, which can present dangers and difficulties. We need, therefore, to be clear at the outset about the sense in which Tolstoy and George understood it. A definition contemporary with Tolstoy runs as follows:

Socialism is that policy or theory which aims at securing *by the action of the central democratic authority* a better distribution, and in due subordination thereunto a better production, of wealth than now prevails.[2]

The nature of the action is not yet certain, but becomes apparent later on:

> ... A great combination approaches monopoly, and a far-reaching, wide-stretching monopoly (say of the carrying trade) might mean a public danger. Should we listen to our friends the socialists and avert the danger by making the state the monopolist?

Our author, James Bonar of Ottawa, appears willing to accept the answer 'Yes'. So would Henry George:

> The primary purpose and end of government being to secure the natural rights and equal liberty of each, all businesses that involve monopoly are within the necessary province of governmental regulation, and businesses that are in their nature complete monopolies become properly functions of the state.[3]

George would have had in mind here such enterprises as railways and postal and telegraph services. The reason for the radical difference between George's estimate and Tolstoy's of the nature of the State could be that, whereas Tolstoy thought mainly of his own corrupt and long-standing autocratic régime, George was a citizen of the United States of America, writing not much more than a hundred years later than the Declaration of Independence. He was conscious of corruption indeed, but had some residual faith in the processes of representative government.

James Bonar might have tolerated state ownership of monopolies; but that is evidently where he would have drawn the line:

> If the ideal of state socialism be viewed in an equally critical spirit, many of the objections brought by the moderate anarchists are seen to have their weight. A strong central government to which all power was given over all the chief industries in the country would, they say, be contrary to liberty. Our leaders would be too

likely to become again our masters. Supervision would become irksome. Great powers would become a temptation to abuse of power.

Events in the Soviet Union were to confirm his judgment.

Tolstoy's objections to socialism were rather more broadly based. In the first place, it would mean more involvement of the State rather than less; so, as was to be expected, he would have rejected it for this reason alone, regardless of what it consisted of in itself:

> Not to mention past attempts to abolish Governments by violence, according to the Socialist theory the coming abolition of the rule of the capitalists, i.e. the communalisation of the means of production, and the new economic order of society, is also to be instituted by a fresh organisation of violence, and will have to be maintained by the same means. So that attempts to abolish violence by violence, neither have in the past, nor, evidently, can in the future, emancipate people from violence, nor, consequently, from slavery.[4]

Tolstoy's foresightedness is evident here. What was Josef Stalin's reaction when he encountered resistance from the kulaks, the successors of the rich peasants who benefited from the post-1861 land purchases, to the new plan to set up collective farms? He had them killed.

But Tolstoy had other objections to socialism. In a chapter in the same work, entitled 'Bankruptcy of the socialist ideal', he argued along these lines. Even if it were to be accepted that town factories were better than village handicrafts (it would seem that by this time he had relaxed his ideal of self-sufficiency, and approved of villages' specialising in certain handicrafts, and exchanging among themselves), there would remain the difficulty that, when the 'means of production' were in the hands of the workers themselves, nobody would know what articles would have to be produced, nor in what quantities. Some of these articles indeed may be considered by some people as useful and necessary, and by others as harmful. Why then should anybody be forced to make them? 'How', he asked, 'in apportioning the work, are people to be induced to agree?' He also thought that the demand for articles of consumption (i.e. wealth) would be limitless: that everybody would want to enjoy all the facilities then enjoyed by the very rich. What a pity that he never had an opportunity to meet, as well as the son, the elder Henry George, who considered, on the contrary, that, if everybody were sure of an adequate material return for labour, nobody would wish to work longer or harder to gain more, but would devote any extra time and energy to pursuits of a higher order. A discussion between them, with Maude there to record it, would have been interesting and enlightening.

On George's side, it could have been pointed out that, when white settlers in Africa wanted to make sure of a regular supply of native labour, they had to create, not only artificial wants in the shape of European clothes, food and drink, but artificial brute necessities in the shape of hut or poll taxes, which had to be paid in European money. An even stronger means of compulsion was the seizure of their land, to prevent their working on their own account. Left to themselves, the natives were liable to work for very short periods of time, and to spend the rest in singing and dancing, or other communal activities.

Henry George, unlike Tolstoy, always assumed the continuance of the State, and admitted that any natural monopoly should be a state monopoly. This accords well with his conception of society as an organic growth in which the free action of the individual is all-important. Any monopoly restricts individual choice; and a private one permits an artificial increase of costs at the general expense. A public one, on the other hand, could at least be subject to public control. Further than this, however, he would not go along the road to socialism, unless it were to come about spontaneously:

> The idea of socialism is grand and noble; and it is, I am convinced, possible of realisation, but such a state of society cannot be manufactured – it must grow. Society is an organism, not a machine. It can only live by the individual life of its parts. And in the free and natural development of all the parts will be secured

the harmony of the whole.[5]

He was to develop this theme more fully in his published reply to the papal encyclical *Rerum Novarum (Concerning Revolution),* which, although it did not refer specifically either to him personally or to his teachings, would probably be interpreted as an attack on them.

After his usual fashion, before criticising an idea adversely, he took care at the outset to define his opponents' position, to state their case for them; so that there should be no question of what he was going to write about. People attacking a case of his were seldom so scrupulous:

> Socialism in all its phases looks on the evils of our civilisation as springing from the inadequacy or inharmony of natural relations, which must be artificially organised or improved. In its idea there devolves on the State the necessity of intelligently organising the industrial relations of men, the construction as it were of a great machine, whose complicated parts shall properly work together under the direction of human intelligence.[6]

This task, however, in his view and in that of his supporters, was impossible. A mechanical human society is beyond our power to devise:

> We see in the natural, social and industrial laws such a harmony as we see in the adjustments of the human body, and that as far transcends the power of man's intelligence to order and direct as it is beyond man's intelligence to order and direct the vital movements of his frame.[7]

Socialists, he considered, were liable to rush into action and apply remedies before they had given adequate thought to what was wrong:

> But it seems to us the vice of Socialism in all its degrees is its want of radicalism, of going to the root ... . It assumes that the tendency of wages to a minimum is the natural law, and seeks to abolish

wages; it assumes that the natural result of competition is to grind down workers, and seeks to abolish competition by restrictions, prohibitions, and extensions of governing power. Thus mistaking effects for causes, and childishly blaming the stone for hitting it, it wastes strength in striving for remedies that when not worse are futile. Associated though it is in many ways with democratic aspiration, yet its essence is the same delusion to which the Children of Israel yielded when, against the protest of their prophet, they insisted on a king; the delusion that has everywhere corrupted democracies and enthroned monarchs – that power over the people can be used for the benefit of the people; that there may be devised machinery that through human agencies will secure for the management of individual affairs more wisdom and more virtue than the people themselves possess.[8]

One would imagine that there could be no two ways of thinking about this matter. Leo Tolstoy and Henry George were not socialists in the generally accepted sense of the word; and Tolstoy, when he became converted to the idea of the single tax, was in no way committing himself to the socialist cause. Neither of them was to become the prophet of the coming revolution, because, apart from any other consideration, they both believed in the slow evolution of human morals and ideas, rather than in any dramatic change.

The man who did in fact become the prophet of the revolution, and of the dictatorship of the proletariat, was Karl Marx. It is a curious reflection on the dissemination of ideas that although, as George remarked, most socialists suffer from a want of radicalism, Marx himself, unlike the majority of his present-day supporters, distinguished carefully between land and capital, and saw clearly that monopoly of the former led to monopoly of the latter:

Labour is not the source of all wealth. Nature is just as much the source of use-values (and of such, to be sure, is material wealth composed) as is labour, which itself is but the expression of natural forces, of human labour power. ... In the society of today, the means of labour monopolized by the landed proprietors, monopoly of landed property is even the basis of monopoly of capital, and by the capitalists.[9]

Nor would he have anything to do with the theory, advanced only in defence of private property in land, that purchase in good faith with honestly earned money is sufficient to secure a valid property right:

> The fact that capitalized ground-rent represents itself as the price or value of land, so that the earth is bought and sold like any other commodity, serves to some apologists as justification of private property in land, seeing that the buyer pays an equivalent for it, the same as he does for other commodities, and that the major portion of property in land has changed hands in this way. The same reason would in that case serve also to justify slavery, since the return from the labour of the slave, whom the slaveholder has bought, represents merely the interest on the capital invested in this purchase. To derive from the sale and purchase of ground-rent a justification of its existence signifies to justify its existence by its existence.[10]

Marx had even, thirty-two years before the publication of Henry George's *Progress and Poverty,* advanced the proposition that all rent should be used for revenue. The first prescription of the *Communist Manifesto* was this:

> Abolition of property in land and application of all rents of land to public purposes.[11]

It would, however, seem from the second prescription, 'a heavy progressive or graduated income tax', that the idea had not occurred to him that the rent of land *alone* would be sufficient for public purposes. Yet a consideration of the implications of Ricardo's law of rent (Ch.11) reveals that taxation as commonly levied cannot possibly bring wages and interest *below* what they would be on the least productive land in use. It only drives labour and capital to operate on land of a higher level of productivity, or, in other words, it encroaches on what would otherwise be rent. Taxation as commonly levied is therefore liable already to be deducted from rent, which would in itself be more than enough for public revenue. Henry George did not state all this explicitly, but seems to have trusted his readers to work it out for themselves.

Unfortunately, the first proposition we have quoted found no place in the first volume of *Das Kapital,* published in 1867, on which Lenin and his fellow revolutionaries based their policies. The continental socialists, like their English counterparts, had 'gone past' – not 'Henry George'; for *Progress and Poverty* had not yet been written – but land value taxation as contemplated by Marx, and 'recognised interest, and private property in the means of production, as being also wrong'. It would have been better for the Union of Soviet Socialist Republics, and later for other countries, if they had resolved to follow Tolstoy and to give the single tax a chance before proceeding to more extreme, but in the end less effective, measures that took no account of the benign as well of the malign potential of economic rent in the life of a community.

Chapter 14
Critics of Tolstoy's Georgism

Whatever tends to preserve the wealth of the wealthy is
called conservatism, and whatever favors anything else, no
matter what, they call socialism.
Richard T. Ely.

A T no time but during the present century has the world
been more in need of prophets to point the way to a saner
and more stable organisation of its affairs. But a prophet relies
on more than his own powers. He needs facilities to disseminate
his teachings, and the services of critics to direct public attention
to them, and, where necessary, by elucidating them, to make
them more available for popular understanding.

It is also the critics' task to warn the people against false
prophets, those whose teachings, if followed, would lead to a
worsening of the state of the world, or even to a major
catastrophe. In this matter they need to take more than usual
care lest they mistake the true for the false, and deprive their
readers, and perhaps eventually the world, of a golden
opportunity. It should therefore be obvious that they
themselves should read what they are setting out to judge,
that skipping to get the general drift will just not do, and that
they should approach their task with a completely open mind.
They need, in fact, to be 'freethinkers' in Tolstoy's sense of the
word.

They need also to bear in mind the regrettable tendency in
university arts courses to overload the syllabus to such an extent
that students are effectively encouraged to trust to the views of
the critics, and to refrain from reading the works criticised.
Once accustomed to this practice, they will carry it into later
life, and may reject unseen at somebody else's behest a work

111

that, if read, would become a valuable part of their way of thinking. So the best critic is the one who not only formulates a right judgment, but encourages his reader to experience personally what he himself has experienced, and to formulate a judgment of his own.

In considering criticisms of Tolstoy's writings on rational Christianity, divorced from the problematic traditional accompaniment of supernatural events, we have encountered a whole range of reactions, from wholehearted acceptance to out and out instinctive rejection. There is little to be done to reconcile these opposing factions, except to hope that one day Christian unity may be founded on an agreement to give priority to Christ's teachings and 'sweet reasonableness', and to differ on the rest. What would help towards such unity is disestablishment, or, in other words, disengagement from the influence of States, and more concentration on the general welfare of mankind.

Tolstoy's strong views on States, based on their propensity to rob, persecute and murder, have always prompted a violent response. This is only to be expected; for the idea of the modern European Nation/State, beginning with the Reformation, and consummated in the unions of both Italy and Germany in the course of the 19th century, is still firmly established in the minds of the majority of people as an acceptable model, despite the evidence of two world wars and continuing political crises. Perhaps, however, it is a hopeful sign that some of his critics felt obliged to resort to such a device as stating or assuming a case that was not Tolstoy's, before commenting sarcastically on it. Other equally dishonest tricks took the form, it will be remembered, of accusing him of failing to prove what he expressly admitted to be unprovable, and of attempting to appeal to the animal instinct of self-defence in a particular situation, whereas what Tolstoy deplored was the general situation that made the question of the need for collective defence even conceivable.

It remains to be seen whether the critics' performance is in any way improved when they come to deal with Tolstoy's final answer, as taken over from Henry George, to the universal question of economic reform. An outstanding example of the depths to which they can descend is furnished by Maude in the shape of comments appearing in *Literature* for the 30th July 1898 on Tolstoy's views about art in general as summed up in his own definition:

> Art is a human activity, consisting in this, that one man consciously, by means of certain external signs, hands on to others feelings he has lived through, and that other people are infected by these feelings and also experience them.[1]

Here is how Maude presents the article from *Literature:*

> For example, a leading article in *Literature* (30th July 1898) accorded to the author of such 'clotted nonsense' 'distinction among aesthetic circle-squarers'. After stating that 'there never was any reason for inferring ... that Count Tolstoi's opinions on the philosophy of art would be worth the paper on which they are written'; and that the expounder of these 'fantastic doctrines surpasses all other advocates of this same theory in perverse unreason', the writer proceeds with an examination of 'the melancholy case of the eminent Russian novelist', and tells us that:

> 'The notion of turning for guidance to a Russian man of letters of whom all we know, outside his literary record, *is that he has embraced Socialism* on much the same grounds of conviction as a Sunday afternoon listener to a Hyde Park orator, and "found religion" in much the same spirit as one of the "Hallelujah lasses" of the Salvation Army, is on the face of it absurd. Nobody, however eminent as a novelist ... has any business to invite his fellow-men to step with him outside the region of sanity ... and sit down beside him like Alice beside the Hatter or the March Hare for the solemn examination of so lunatic a thesis as this'.[2]

The thesis appears sensible enough; but, that apart, what possible reason could the writer have had for thinking that Tolstoy had 'embraced Socialism' on any 'grounds of conviction' whatever, let alone 'found religion' after the fashion of the

Salvation Army? Both statements are palpably untrue; and the only remaining subject for speculation is whether the writer made them out of his own state of abysmal ignorance, or in comfortable certainty about the reader's.

Most slurs on Tolstoy and his thought in the realm of political economy are cast in the first instance, however, on Henry George and his single tax, and then, by implication, on Tolstoy for his belief in them. The chief exponent of this kind of attack is Henri Troyat, who writes as follows:

Nekhlyudov had tried to carry out a bloodless revolution among the peasants on his own estate. Thus, after lending his agricultural theories of one period to Levin in *Anna Karenina,* Tolstoy now bestows his latest views on the subject upon the hero of *Resurrection.* Inspired by the the American socialist Henry George, Nekhlyudov favours a single land tax, high enough to compel the large owners to cede their land to the State. The tax would abolish private property and the State would redistribute the nationalized land among all the peasants who cultivated it. It is odd that Neklyudov (alias Tolstoy) should have been so hypnotized by this pseudo-communistic utopia that he failed to realize that in order to carry out such a redistribution it would first be necessary to change the government, or in other words, to make a radical and presumably bloody political reform.[3]

And again:

'... He was full of plans: articles on the religious question, a message to the young, a commentary on Henry George's theories of agricultural reform.[4]

These passages call for a few comments. Henry George was not a socialist. There is no question in his books of ceding land to the State, let alone of the State's redistribution of it. 'Pseudo-communistic utopia' is a cheap and meaningless sneer. George, as we have seen (Ch.12), specifically denied that his measure could be implemented by means of revolution, 'bloody' or not. He did not write about the reform of agriculture, but about redistributing taxation so that it should fall only on the value of land, all land. In a nutshell, Troyat did not understand Henry George's philosophy, and is therefore ill-equipped to criticise it.

A.N. Wilson does not become so excited about Tolstoy's economic views as he used to about his religious ones, but he too shows a lack of understanding when he deals with them:

> ... The majority of the population of the Empire were peasant farmers, who merely wanted to farm their land in peace, owning their own property and harbouring their own profits. Tolstoy could not approve of them because he regarded it as an *a priori* truth, culled from the writings of Henry George, that land should be in public ownership. But public ownership implies an all-powerful state, and Tolstoy did not want that either.[5]

And again:

> ... But Tolstoy's later diaries are stupendously tedious full of the usual old reflections about Henry George's land tax, the moral beauties of Chertkov, the love of God and the hell of family life.[6]

Henry George wrote: *'We must make land common property'.*[7] He proposed to achieve this solely by using its rent for public revenue, and envisaged as a result of this purely fiscal reform a situation in which the State would be less powerful, not more, as Wilson seems to think. It is not hard to imagine the progression of events. With the introduction of the single tax, land-holding in itself would become unprofitable, and land would gravitate into the hands of those who proposed to use it most efficiently. There would then be no further reason why the demand for goods of all kinds should not stimulate their supply. Unemployment, together with the low wages induced by competition for jobs, would become phenomena of purely historical interest. With unemployment and poverty there would also diminish poverty-related domestic unrest and crime, and with them any excuse for the existence of the police and the army as instruments of internal coercion.

Assuming for the moment the hypothesis of a simultaneous

world-wide application of Georgist principles, we can also be reasonably certain that fighting for land would come to an end, together with fighting for foreign markets in which to sell goods unsaleable at home. Thus would vanish the second excuse for the existence of national armies. On the more likely hypothesis of the adoption of Georgist principles by one country alone, it is possible, even probable if the histories of the French and Russian revolutions are anything to go by, that it would have to face attack from the rest, and would need to retain its armed forces. They would at least be fighting for a common interest, instead of for concealed special ones, and should prove hard to beat. They would also be associations of free men, like the Roman armies of the early republic or even more so, but certainly not instruments in the hands of 'an all-powerful state'. Tolstoy's initial hesitations about the single tax were based mainly on the grounds of its requiring even a single measure of state action. It would appear that none of these things is of much concern to Wilson, whose level of comprehension outside the realm of pure literature, if there is such a thing, is adequately revealed by his prep school use of the word 'old' in 'the usual old reflections'.

Finally, the expression 'a priori truth' is grossly misleading. Wilson is evidently not aware that George reached his conclusions about private property in land as the result of careful and logical arguments. He too is insufficiently familiar with George's works to be entitled to criticise them.

E.J. Simmons' judgment is equally dubious:

> ... First attracted by *Progress and Poverty,* Tolstoy read other works of George, began to comment on him in his writings as early as 1884, and devoted articles to his ideas. He also advocated his plan for the abolition of private property in land and the single tax to all who would listen and corresponded with George whose visit to Yasnaya Polyana was prevented only by the American's death. There were weaknesses in his theorizing, which Tolstoy felt did not go far enough, but he regarded the plan as a practical answer to the festering sore in the economic body of Russia – the land hunger of the peasantry. Though he thought of George's

nostrum as at best a compromise and regretted that the tax would be collected by a government based on violence, he was willing to accept these disadvantages because the greater good of the greater number would be served.[8]

Tolstoy was first attracted by *Social problems,* not *Progress and poverty.* What were the weaknesses in George's theorising? When George himself found weaknesses in other people's theorising, he took the trouble to quote the relevant passages, and to point out exactly what he considered to be wrong. This is the only satisfactory procedure. In what respect did Tolstoy think that George's theorising did not go far enough? Surely we are entitled to know. Or is this just another method of 'rubbishing' Henry George? The use of the word 'nostrum', defined in *Chambers's Twentieth Century Dictionary* as 'any secret, quack or patent medicine', certainly is. The most likely effect of all this is to instil prejudice into the uninstructed reader, and dissuade him from reading Henry George's works for himself.

Theodore Redpath also is an expert in the use of the pejorative term. He writes:

... The book *Resurrection* advocates nationalization of the land and the imposition of a single tax, according to the system of Henry George. That would have caused a drift back to the land.[9]

Nationalization of the land' is an utterly misleading description of what George proposed. As generally understood, it implies some scheme of compensation, to which George, for adequately explained reasons, was totally opposed. It would also involve an extension of the bureaucracy, whereas he considered that the allocative function would better be left to the operations of the free market. It is true that his single tax would have the effect of bringing on to the market at a lowered price rural land unused, or inadequately used, by its existing titular owners, thus offering opportunities for engaging in agriculture to those who would otherwise be prevented from so doing. It is hardly fair to describe such a purposeful process as a 'drift'.

After such loaded and prejudiced accounts of Tolstoy's conversion to the idea of Henry George's single tax, it comes as a relief to read some that are at least neutral in tone. Perhaps their very neutrality may be interpreted as tacit acceptance. Here is Victor Shklovsky, who, as a citizen of the Union of Soviet Socialist Republics, might be expected to approve of a doctrine that had appeared in the *Communist Manifesto* of 1847. The first four words refer to Tolstoy's anarchism:

> No government was needed, and yet it appeared that the liberation of land which must take place could be best accomplished by order of the Tsar. Though the Tsar was young, muddled, and afraid of his relatives, he still might issue a decree on the liberation of land, This decree supported by the introduction of a single land tax which would make the private ownership of large acreages unprofitable.
>
> There was an error in the logic here: a government was not needed but an act of government was; there would be opposition to the land reform, and the opposition would have to be combated, but not by force. Persuasion was the only acceptable means of struggle.[10]

And further on:

> His project of land reform after Henry George was not accepted. It was of no use to the peasants now that they had nearly redeemed their allotments. Exorbitant though the price was, they had paid it out.[11]

This is a perceptive comment. The peasants who had 'nearly redeemed their allotments' as a result of the settlement of 1861 were in effect about to join the ranks of the landowning class, privileged to receive rent as well as wages. They would certainly be opposed to George's reform, regardless of the cost to the future generations of people who were to be denied access to land. For the condition of these unfortunates would not only never be improved by such a half-measure as that of 1861, it could even be worsened. Here is Henry George on the subject, discussing the situation in France and Belgium, where similar redistributions of land had taken place during the French Revolution:

> Just what may be accomplished by the greater division of land may be seen in those districts of France and Belgium where minute division prevails. That such a division of land is on the whole much better, and that it gives a far more stable basis to the state than that which prevails in England, there can be no doubt. But that it does not make wages any higher or improve the condition of the class who have only their labour, is equally clear. These French and Belgian peasants practise a rigid economy unknown to any of the English-speaking peoples. And if such striking symptoms of the poverty and distress of the lowest class are not apparent as on the other side of the channel, it must, I think, be attributed, not only to this fact, but to another fact, which accounts for the continuance of the minute division of the land – that material progress has not been so rapid.

> Neither has population increased with the same rapidity (on the contrary it has been nearly stationary), nor have improvements in the modes of production been so great. Nevertheless, M. de Lave-leye, all of whose prepossessions are in favour of small holdings, and whose testimony will therefore carry more weight than that of English observers, who may be supposed to harbour a prejudice for the system of their own country, states in his paper on the Land Systems of Belgium and Holland printed by the Cobden Club, that the condition of the labourer is worse under this system of the minute division of land than it is in England; while the tenant farmers – for tenancy largely prevails even where the *morcellement* is greatest – are rack-rented with a mercilessness unknown in England, and even in Ireland, and the franchise 'so far from raising them in the social scale, is but a source of mortification and humiliation to them, for they are forced to vote according to the dictates of the landlord instead of following the dictates of their own inclinations and convictions'.[12]

Shklovsky hints at the existence of the same state of affairs in Russia, caused by the same mistaken reform:

> ... there was a community with re-allotments of land, but within the community itself there were peasants who owned no land at all, peasants with miserable allotments, and kulaks who hired labour and rented land.[13]

Another neutral commentator is Henry Gifford:

> ... He became an ardent advocate of the contemporary American economist and reformer Henry George's Single Tax on land, which Nekhlyudov in *Resurrection* expounds to his peasants (II ix): 'He had a head on him, that Zhorzha', says one. But again, when pressed on this by Aylmer Maude, he was forced to admit that the system required a government to administer it, and ideally he stood against all governments. The need to be consistent caused him much anxiety. However, the Sermon on the Mount is nothing but a series of hard choices, and its recommendations are drastic.[14]

Is this tacit acceptance? Or can we take Gifford's choice of quotation from *Resurrection* as being more than this? In either case, it has to be admitted that neither he nor Shklovsky has performed for the reader the basic task of giving an adequate explanation of what it was that Henry George was advocating, or of why it was that Tolstoy was so attracted to it.

The same has to be said, unfortunately, about Aylmer Maude, the Boswell to Tolstoy's Johnson. In *Talks with Tolstoy*,[15] he is concerned to reconcile with Tolstoy's anarchism the need for government of some sort to implement the single tax. If there must be laws, then let them be good ones, is the view he attributes to his friend. He also takes pains to describe Tolstoy's reaction to the initial slow progress of the single tax in England. Further than this he does not go. In the biography, he has a curiously ambiguous statement to make:

> ... George's *Social Problems* and *Progress and Poverty*, with their

deep feeling, lucid statement, broad outlook, indignation at existing inequalities, and absence of practical administrative detail, were books just calculated to secure his warm sympathy.[16]

This is true enough in the main; but the hint that neither Tolstoy nor George was a practical man could be damaging. And, after all, would one have expected George to produce a blueprint that would be universally applicable? What he does have to say on the subject of practicalities is as follows:

Nor to take rent for public uses is it necessary that the State should bother with the letting of lands, and assume the chances of the favouritism, collusion, and corruption this might involve. It is not necessary that any new machinery should be created. The machinery already exists. Instead of extending it, all we have to do is to simplify and reduce it. By leaving to land owners a percentage of rent which would probably be much less than the cost and loss involved in attempting to rent lands through State agency, and by making use of this existing machinery, we may, without jar or shock, assert the common right to land by taking rent for public uses.[17]

In the face of this, what is one to make of such assertions as Troyat's '... the State would redistribute the nationalized land ...'? Are they examples of ignorance or of intentional misrepresentation? We may say nowadays that George's scheme would do well enough for a first tentative step, but that it might eventually lead to some system of public auctions with rents being bid instead of prices. Nevertheless, this is no excuse for attributing to George ideas that he never contemplated.

In extenuation of Maude, however, it must be said that he does his best by Tolstoy in quoting an account by the peasant/ author Semëmov of a conversation he had had with Tolstoy on the subject of landholding. Unfortunately, it would seem that Semëmov had not perfectly understood what the Master was talking about:

'But would such a tax not be too heavy for those who work the land'?

'Not at all! *The tax would be as much as the land would yield without labour by its fertility and nearness to a market. If it would yield pasture for three rubles, that would be the tax.* If a market was near at hand so that one could get a good revenue from having a market-garden, one would have to pay more, and if the land was in the chief street in Moscow one would have to pay a great deal for it, but it would be quite fair, for it is not the owner who gives land its value but the whole community, and the community would only take back what is rightly its own!'[18]

It is of course a mistake to say that the 'fertility and nearness to a market' of a piece of land would yield anything at all without labour. What would have been true to say is that the tax would represent the advantage attributable to exceptional fertility and nearness to a market. It is to be feared that Maude's uncritical repetition of this lapse shows that his own grasp of the subject was on the weak side.

On the whole, we have to acknowledge that the message of this particular sample of opinions is that Tolstoy was not well served by his critics in the matter of his contribution to political economy. Although it is only a small sample, it is probably representative enough; for writers on literary topics are not noted for their familiarity with the works of Henry George.

Victor Shklovsky finishes his book with a moving tribute. After telling the story of Samson and the Philistines, he concludes as follows:

The grief, the wrath, and the awakening of the people have all found their expression in the great creations of Lev Tolstoy.

All his life, the people he lived among urged him to be sensible, but he was one of those who shook the pillars of their temples.[19]

The temples fell in Russia and elsewhere, only to be replaced by others, which have now been shaken in their turn. The present generation bears the responsibility of rebuilding them so that they will last.

Chapter 15
Land value taxation in action

His form and cause conjoined, preaching to stones
would make them capable.
Shakespeare.

W E saw in Ch.12 that Tolstoy had made an attempt in
1902, via the Grand Duke Nikolay Mikhaylovich, to
interest the Tsar Nicholas II in the idea of land reform, and that
entries in his personal diary for the 20th and 28th August 1909
show him talking to members of the Duma on the same subject.
All three efforts, and possibly others unrecorded, ended in
failure, for one excellent reason. Nation/States were then all
ruled in the interests of people whose wealth had been
consolidated or created as a consequence of extensive unconditional landownership. They were therefore resistant to any
change calculated to secure a radical and permanent redistribution of wealth away from them.

Much the same thing was happening in England,[1] where the
Liberal Party came into office in 1906 largely because their
programme included land value taxation. The popular feeling in
favour of it may be judged from the fact that no fewer than 173
M.P.s signed a petition late in May 1911 demanding immediate
action. These men were, of course, thinking about their
constituencies and the next election; but the Cabinet had also
to think about the influential people who provided a substantial
proportion of the party funds. Being above all adroit politicians,
they managed to say enough in public about the iniquity of
landlordism to hold the land value taxers in check, while at the
same time satisfying the landowners with their masterly
inactivity. Here is the Prime Minister himself, H.H. Asquith,
at the head of an administration with a clear mandate to tax

124

land values, talking on the subject at Ladybank on the 5th October 1912:

'The government ... will not embrace what is called the policy of the single tax, which to my knowledge has not a single supporter in the present Cabinet, which ... is consistent neither with justice nor with expediency'.[2]

There is no need to be surprised: such equivocation is part of the common currency of what is known as statesmanship. As a result of this particular specimen, and of obstruction in the House of Lords, only watered-down measures had reached the Statute Book by 1914, when the war broke out. Nothing more was then done; and even what legislation had been achieved was repealed in 1922; and payments were refunded. The background to the affair has been spelt out as follows:

... Seventy per cent of the entire adult population was excluded from the polls. The numbers returned by this restricted suffrage were a social as well as a political élite. In the House of Commons of 1906, 81 per cent of Conservatives and 73 per cent of Liberals had as their major economic interest landowning or commerce and industry. Of Liberals 33 per cent, of Conservatives 51 per cent had attended a public school; 36 per cent of both parties had been educated at Oxford or Cambridge. Two per cent of Liberals and no Conservatives were trade unionists. The socio-economic background of the Cabinet, and of under secretaries of state, was even more exclusive than that of M.P.s.[3]

One must record with regret the failure of this attempt to establish a Georgist experiment nationally in a country whose world-wide influence was still strong, and whose example might have been followed. In other places, however, particularly those where English-speaking colonists were recovering, or had already recovered, from the dead hand of land and capital monopoly in the mother country, and had not yet completely succumbed to the home-grown variety of it, limited experiments have been carried out, in the fields of local and national taxation and the financing of special undertakings. The results have naturally not been such as to fulfil all Henry George's expectations; but they nevertheless encourage confidence that his is the right way towards ultimate economic justice.

In New Zealand, for example, it had become obvious to the settlers, even before Henry George wrote *Progress and poverty*, that the installation of public amenities, paid for out of the rates, increased the value of vacant sites just as much as it did those of sites that had been built on. It seemed to them, therefore, entirely rational that the rates should be based on the value of the land alone. A visit by Henry George in 1890 merely confirmed their views.

The central authorities thought otherwise, with the result that, when practice was consolidated nationally by a law of 1896, the system of rating prescribed was based on the combined value of land and buildings. Despite this, the feeling in favour of land value rating was so strong that an escape clause had to be inserted. If 15 per cent of the ratepayers asked for it, a poll or referendum could be held, as a result of which a simple majority deciding in favour of it could effect the change. By 1988, 81 per cent of the local authorities were using land value rating.

The effect that it could have on the development of a city is aptly illustrated by the contrast between Auckland, where rating has always been carried out on the basis of a putative annual rental value of both buildings and land, as it was in Britain until 1990, and Wellington, where a change to land value rating was made in 1902. In 1986,[4] for every $100 worth of land in Auckland, there was $144 worth of buildings; but, in Wellington, there was $240 worth! Whereas Auckland is a picture of dereliction, Wellington was self-renewing, that is, redundant buildings would be removed immediately to make room for something more useful. It does not require much imagination to see that the effects of this would be felt beyond the building trade. Where there is an annual charge on the value of a site, buildings will not be put up unless they are going to be used, which implies more employment of other kinds. And the nearer the approach that is made to full employment, the more will wages approximate to the full value created by labour, as Henry George discovered in San Francisco at the time of the Frazer River gold rush.

Since 1986, the central authorities of New Zealand have been working on behalf of those occupiers of inner city sites who find land value rating little to their taste. The poll was abolished as from the 1st April 1988; and the choice between rating on land and buildings or on land alone was vested unconditionally in local councils. Wellington City Council was the first to change back. The way is now open, and is being used, for property owners going out of business to remove the roofs from their buildings, and to continue to pay tax on the land alone, but at the lower rate appropriate to land and buildings. They hope eventually to sell the land at a profit that will more than compensate for the tax they have paid in the meantime.

Dr Steven Cord, late of the University of Indiana, U.S.A., and a tireless advocate of land value rating in the cities of Pennsylvania, has made a useful compendium of evidence, comparable to that regarding Auckland and Wellington, that 'shifting the property tax off buildings onto land values has ... been followed by new construction'.[5] He drew his material from records of local revenue raising in Pennsylvania, Australia and the Republic of South Africa.

An outstanding example is that of Pittsburgh (Pa). The City Council there still taxes buildings as well as land, but has been taxing land at a higher rate in the dollar since 1913. Between 1925 and 1979, the rate on land was always at least double that on buildings; but then it was increased to nearly four times. By 1987, after repeated changes, it stood at 5.6 times. If the four years (1974-78) before the major change are compared with the four years after (1980-84), we learn that the value of building permits issued increased in Pittsburgh by a factor of 5.9, but in the United States as a whole by only 1.6.

Another body of researchers has compared the average sale prices of new and existing homes in twenty-four American cities. The figures were obtained from the Federal Home Loan Bank Board in January 1988, and range from $229,300 in Boston to $51,300 in Pittsburgh. The explanation is simple. Where there is a sufficiently high tax on the value of land, sellers are eager to sell and buyers have more choice. As a result there are relatively lower land prices and correspondingly lower ones for houses. The final effect is visible. This is what our authors have to say about the general housing situation in the United States:

> New waves of homeless people are appearing daily. Soaring rents and housing prices are pushing even many of the working poor and families with children into the ranks of the homeless.[6]

Even in Pittsburgh, there were until recently publicly financed shelters for the homeless. In the *Washington Post* for the 4th April 1990, however, it was reported that 'shelters in Pittsburgh are being closed', because it is 'rare to see someone sleeping on downtown streets'. The inhabitants of Pittsburgh have been enabled by the two-rate property tax to catch up on their shortfall of adequate places to live.

Spurts in building construction have followed a local tax shift to land values in other Pennsylvanian cities besides Pittsburgh. McKeesport, for example, adopted the two-rate tax in 1980, whereas comparable DuQuesne and Clairton did not. During the next two years, the value of building permits issued in McKeesport increased by 38 per cent over that for the preceding two; but there were falls in DuQuesne and Clairton of 20 and 28 per cent respectively. History repeated itself two years later in New Castle, where a gain of 70 per cent was recorded for the years 1982-85, as against losses of 66 and 90 per cent in Farrell and Sharon. Similarly, two-rate Scranton out-performed the neighbouring city of Wilkes-Barre. Encouraged by these examples, more and more Pennsylvanian cities are adopting the two-rate tax – fifteen at the time of writing (1991); and some are even contemplating a local tax on land value alone.

Similarly favourable results have followed in Australia from the introduction of a local property tax based on land value alone, to replace one on both land and buildings. In the rural shire of Buninyong, to name one example, the change was introduced in April 1972 on the initiative of the local taxpayers, most of whom were farmers and cattlemen. From then until

1978, the value represented by the annual issue of building permits increased from $1,897 to $7,087, the first figure covering three months of taxed and nine months of un-taxed buildings. During the previous three years, the value had been falling from $415 to $393.

In the Republic of South Africa, a survey of the 125 biggest towns shows a movement away from a flat-rate tax on both land and buildings to a two-rate tax in the style of Pennsylvania, and from that to a pure land value tax. Towns in the first category, from 1959 to 1979, increased their total building assessments by 486 per cent, in the second by 561 per cent, but in the third by 850 per cent. Those moving during the period from category one to category two recorded an increase of 748 per cent; but those moving from two to three did best of all with a staggering increase of 996 per cent.

One of the men mainly responsible for introducing land value rating into South Africa was the late Hon. Frank A.W. Lucas, Q.C. He recalled that, when he was a student at Cape Town, the Professor of English told the class that, although their essays were not bad, they showed no signs of original thought. He then suggested that it would stimulate their thinking if they were to read Henry George's *Progress and Poverty*. Lucas did not actually do so until about nine years later; but, when he did, he was struck, as Tolstoy had been, with the potential of the land value tax for solving our political, social and economic problems. Elected in 1914 to the Transvaal Provincial Council, he introduced and had passed, as leader of the Labour majority, an ordinance giving local authorities power to rate site values only, and to exempt all buildings. When the system was well established, he expressed the opinion that it would take a dictator to change it. It is ironic that, in a country where a beneficent land reform is steadily gaining support in the urban areas, there should still be strife over land-ownership in the open country, where the bitterness occasioned by old wars is still as alive as ever. Perhaps the example of the cities will in time point the way to a sane solution of the whole land problem.

Denmark is another country where the ideas of Henry

George have had some influence, particularly in the matter of free trade.[7] During the years 1875 to 1895, the falling price of grain was alleged to be the cause of the devastation of British agriculture; but, in Denmark, the peasantry, determined to take advantage of this very fall, resisted all attempts to impose import duties, and used cheap grain from America as raw material for the production of milk, butter, cheese, bacon and eggs. They made this same ruinous period one of great prosperity for them. The idea of land value taxation has had, and still has, a place in the political life of the Danes; but, although they have established an exemplary system of land valuation, the rate of tax actually levied has been far too small to have any significant effect.

Much more dramatic have been the results of land value taxation related to a specific type of expenditure in California, where the state legislature determined, in 1887, to create Irrigation Districts, so financed, for the purpose of retaining and distributing water during the rainless summer months. The result was the replacement of large, semi-desert areas, exploited only by the cattle barons, with small holdings of which the typical size is about 30 acres. No further state action was necessary.

So far we have considered only applications of Henry George's theory within the existing social framework; but there is never a lack of persons who, when they learn of a new theory, immediately think in terms of forming a miniature community based on it, and cut off as far as possible from society at large. Tolstoy's earlier ideas of self-sufficiency and abolition of all individual property rights were particularly tempting to such people, who set up numerous 'Tolstoyan' colonies, including two English ones at Croydon and Purleigh. Information available up to the beginning of Mikhail Gorbachev's policy of *glasnost* or 'openness' suggested that they all failed, mainly because their members discovered that personal property is very hard to forego. To do Tolstoy justice, he never recommended any such organisations. For example, we are told that, in July 1896, he wrote as follows to a certain John Kenworthy concerning the projected colony at Purleigh:

... I think that a great deal of the evil of the world is due to our wishing to see the realisation of what we are striving at *but are not yet ready for,* and our being therefore satisfied with the semblance of that which should be ... . We are so created that we cannot become perfect either one by one or in groups, but (from the very nature of the case) only all together.[8]

The latest information (1991) suggests that Tolstoyan pragmatists are still, despite the unfortunate record, attempting to set up such groups.

Georgist colonies are fewer in number, and make no demands on their members in the way of unusual life-style. Typical examples in the U.S.A. are the Fairhope Single Tax Corporation,[9] founded in 1894, and the three Ardens,[10] namely Arden, Ardentown and Ardencroft, founded in 1900, 1922 and 1950 respectively. Roughly speaking, the arrangement is that the corporate bodies own the land, and the tenants' rent goes to pay outside taxes that they would otherwise owe. Such organisations are not, and cannot be regarded as, critical experiments in Georgist theory; for no before-and-after statistics can be produced, nor can meaningful comparisons be made with neighbouring, non-Georgist, communities. Nevertheless, they make no intrusions on the private lives of their inhabitants, and have pleased them all except a minority who wish to convert their leaseholds to freeholds, with a view to future windfall gains in land value. Attempts by such people to dispute the legality of the bodies' constitutions have failed; and the bodies themselves all continue in existence. This in itself is something for them to be proud of.

Chapter 16
War: the useless remedies

*The world organization debates disarmament in one room
and, in the next room, moves the knights and pawns that
make national arms imperative.*
E.B. White.

W E have already seen Tolstoy inveighing against the
vested interests, and the States supporting them, that
had led to both the Boer War and the Russo-Japanese War
within a few years of each other (Ch.6). But he did more than
comment on the international affairs current during the last
decade of his life: he ventured on predictions for the future,
comparing the Christian world of his time with a man who has
missed the right turning and carried on regardless, but becomes
conscious of a precipice ahead:

> That is where Christian humanity stands in our time. It is quite
> evident that if we continue to live as we are doing – guided in our
> private lives and in the lives of our separate states solely by desire
> for personal welfare for ourselves or our states, and think, as we
> now do, to ensure this welfare by violence – then the means for
> violence of man against man and state against state will inevitably
> increase, and we shall first ruin ourselves more and more by
> expending a major portion of our productivity on armaments, and
> then become more and more degenerate and depraved by killing
> the physically best men in wars.

> If we do not change our way of life this is as certain as it is
> mathematically certain that two non-parallel straight lines must
> meet. And not only is it certain theoretically, but in our time our
> feeling as well as our intelligence becomes convinced of it. The

132

precipice we are approaching is already visible, and even the most simple, naïve, and uneducated people cannot fail to see that by arming ourselves increasingly against one another and slaughtering one another in war, we must inevitably come to mutual destruction, like spiders in a jar.

A sincere, serious, and rational man can now no longer console himself with the thought that matters can be mended, as was formerly supposed, by a universal empire such as that of Rome, or Charlemagne, or Napoleon, or by the medieval, spiritual power of the Pope, or by alliances, the political balance of a European concert and peaceful international tribunals, or as some have thought by an increase of military forces and the invention of new and more powerful weapons of destruction.[1]

Universal empires and the spiritual power of the Pope are probably no longer under serious consideration as solutions to the problem of the peaceful governance of the world, and need not concern us here. Alliances, however, are another matter, and are worth some careful thought. Was Tolstoy right? As he delivered this judgment of their uselessness for the purpose of preventing war, he was probably thinking of an effort that he himself had once made in a small way to discourage the negotiations leading to the one between France and Russia that contributed so largely to the fatal events of July 1914. We owe our knowledge of this incident to the record kept by Anna Seuron, a Frenchwoman who was governess to the family from 1882 to 1888.

It was in 1886 that Paul Déroulède, who had come to Russia to arrange the preliminaries, decided, out of a spirit of curiosity, to visit the literary giant at Yasnaya Polyana. The meeting between the apostle of non-violence and the author of *Chants du Soldat (The Soldier's Songs)* was friendly enough; but the visitor had nobody on his side when he said that he hoped another war would soon bring about the reunion of Alsace/Lorraine with France. He was further disappointed when he expressed a wish to hear what the peasants had to say on the subject of the projected alliance. Tolstoy introduced him to some of them out in the fields, and asked them to say what they thought of the idea of fighting the Germans as allies of the French. 'What for?', replied one of them, named Prokopy. 'Let the Frenchman come work with us, and bring the German along with him. When we've finished we'll go for a walk. And we'll take the German with us. He's a man like all the rest'.[2] Déroulèdewas decidedly not pleased.

The French had another motive, besides the recovery of Alsace/Lorraine, to fight a successful war with Germany – namely, the growing German commercial ambitions in Africa.[3] Past differences with Britain were settled in 1904 by an agreement that, in return for French consent to a predominantly British influence in Egypt, a considerable source of raw material for the cotton industry, the British would not interfere with French interests in Morocco, largely to do with the mining of iron ore. Besides this, it is noteworthy that Britain was Morocco's most considerable trading partner, and would not wish to see German influence there on the increase.

The new-found solidarity, not defined by a formal alliance, but reinforced by army and navy staff talks, was first put to the test in 1911, two years after a Franco-German agreement intended to secure the 'political interests' of France in Morocco, so long as France would safeguard Germany's 'economic equality'. The German firm of Mannesmann Brothers had acquired certain mining rights, which the French did not recognise, because they conflicted with the claims of the international Union des Mines Marocaines. At the same time, the French continued to tighten their grip on the country with police and soldiers, who probably had little comprehension of what was at stake. Things came to a head in 1911 with a revolt by Moroccan chieftains, during which Fez was occupied by French troops.

The Germans chose to regard this action as an abrogation of the two-year-old agreement, and sent the gunboat *Panther* into the port of Agadir. Their ostensible reason was to protect German 'interests'; but their real reason was to have a strong bargaining position from which to demand compensation elsewhere if the French were to establish a protectorate over

Morocco. Here the British trading 'interests' came to the rescue, using Lloyd George as a mouthpiece. He made it clear, in his famous Mansion House speech, that, in any contest, Britain would side with France. After digesting this information, the Germans assumed a more conciliatory attitude, and accepted the idea of the French protectorate in return for compensation in the form of more than 100,000 square miles of the French Congo. War had been narrowly averted on this occasion; but one feels that, if Tolstoy had still been alive, he would have been entitled to point out that, despite his public warnings, the same forces that he had identified as causes of war were still operating, but even more dangerously, and that, on the next occasion, the Franco-British informal alliance would have fatal consequences.

The Russo-Japanese war had not affected Russian imperialist ambitions far to the south-west, also based on the exploitation of other peoples' land, as Tolstoy had observed. One project was a concession to build a railway from the Russian border to Teheran, the Persian capital, and to prospect along it for oil and coal.[4] This kind of effort would have been a natural object of suspicion to British imperialists, for whom the whole Middle East was of the utmost importance as a first line of defence to shield their Indian interests – chiefly the sale there of cotton and iron – from European rivals. Nor was the suspicion without foundation. In 1906, however, it so happened that Russian foreign affairs were taken over by Alexander Izvolski, who believed that Russia and Britain should be allies rather than enemies. He had good reason for this, granted the assumptions of the multi-handed game of 'national interests'; for, after the accession of Kaiser Wilhelm II, it became apparent that German 'interests' were bent on monopolising Turkey as a sphere of influence. So in 1907 there was signed an agreement between Britain and Russia, effecting a settlement of their rival interests in Persia, Afghanistan and Tibet.

Of more immediate relevance to the outbreak of the First World War was the Russians' long-standing aim of gaining control of the Dardanelles, and, as a consequence, obtaining access to the Mediterranean for their Black Sea fleet. This, from the point of view of the rulers of the Austro-Hungarian Empire, would have been a disaster to be averted at all costs, even that of a war, in which, after all, they would have the Germans on their side. They were also deeply involved in the repression of their subject peoples, and the retention of that valuable asset, tempting to the Russians, of the oilfields of Galicia.

It must have been a realistic assessment of the probability, amounting to certainty, of Germany's supporting Austria that led the Russian administration and General Staff to order and formulate a plan of mobilisation directed against both countries simultaneously. A last minute attempt at a partial mobilisation against Austria alone would, as a result, have caused inextricable confusion. So the Russian general mobilisation, set in motion on the 30th July 1914 as a counter-move to the Austrian invasion of Serbia, brought about the suspension of German efforts to restrain their allies, and the immediate implementation of the German war plan for an initial rapid campaign against France. Izvolski's reported exclamation of 'C'est ma guerre!' ('*It's my war!*') must have been substantially true. Is it possible to doubt, in the light of these calamities, that Tolstoy was right about alliances? Far from preventing wars, they help them to spread.

If Paul Déroulède had taken the trouble to explain to Tolstoy's peasant-friend Prokopy what he knew of the economic and political background to the proposed alliance, would the latter have been more interested in the idea of joining the French to fight against the Germans? It is hardly likely. Nor, it is to be imagined, would the run-of-the-mill Englishman, burdened with the same knowledge, have rushed to join the colours with quite the same enthusiasm that in fact he showed, unless indeed it was the prospect of regular square meals that constituted the main inducement. Luckily for the British authorities, there was no need for them to reveal the true facts, namely that they were defending, and perhaps even hoping to augment, British interests in Africa and elsewhere. They made the most instead of the German infringement of Belgian neutrality.

When the war was over, the real motives on the allied side

were revealed by the recovery of Alsace/Lorraine and the confiscation of the German colonies. This last had already been provided for, while the war was still in progress, by a secret agreement that also was to permit a Russian occupation of Constantinople, and the long hoped-for freedom of access to the Mediterranean. The Russian defeat and the separate peace treaty of Brest-Litovsk, however, put an end to this hope.

In the meantime, the former fighting men themselves were entertaining doubts about the validity of the causes for which they had fought. The most notable of them was the German Erich Maria Remarque, of whose novel *Im Westen Nichts Neues* *(All Quiet on the Western Front)* 300,000 copies were printed in England in the one year of 1929. Here are the narrator Paul Bäumer's reflections on a group of Russian prisoners of war – were they not the counterparts of Tolstoy's peasant-friend Prokopy? – on whom he is standing guard:

I see their dark forms, their beards move in the wind. I know nothing of them except that they are prisoners; and that is exactly what troubles me. Their life is obscure and guiltless; – if I could know more of them, what their names are, how they live, what they are waiting for, what are their burdens, then my emotion would have an object and might become sympathy. But as it is I perceive behind them only the suffering of the creature, the awful melancholy of life and the pitilessness of men.

A word of command has made these silent figures our enemies; a word of command might transform them into our friends. *At some table a document is signed by some persons whom none of us knows, and then for years together that very crime on which formerly the world's condemnation and severest penalty fell, becomes our highest aim.* But who can draw such a distinction when he looks at these quiet men with their childlike faces and apostles' beards! Any non-commissioned officer is more of an enemy to a recruit, any schoolmaster to a pupil, than they are to us. And yet we would shoot at them again and they at us if they were free.[5]

The italicised portion could have been written by Tolstoy

himself: the offhand contemptuous reference to the political processes would have been typical. So would have been the implication that war is murder. Perhaps Remarque did read some of Tolstoy's anti-State, anti-war writings. What is certain is that the inter-war Nazi Germany became too hot to hold him, and that he took refuge in the United States, eventually marrying Paulette Goddard, the former wife of Charles Chaplin, another free-thinker. He became an American citizen in 1947.

Alliances had been shown to be no guarantee of world order; but would 'the political balance of a European concert and peaceful international tribunals' fare any better? The experiment of the former is only just (1991) being set up; and the idea of a common monetary system is already causing much disagreement. However, we can only wait and see. The precise concept of a tribunal to replace war has never actually been put into practice, though one cannot but agree with Tolstoy's comment that immediately follows the passage quoted: 'But who would impose obedience to the tribunal's decision on a contending party that had an army of millions of men?' Who indeed! However, the Covenant of the League of Nations, established after the First World War, was a plan along the same lines, and deserves some detailed attention.

These were its provisions. First and foremost, each member nation had to 'undertake to respect and preserve as against external aggression the territorial integrity and existing political independence of all members of the League'. After accepting this undertaking, they had as individuals the right to report to either the Council or the Assembly any happenings likely to threaten peace, and the obligation not to resort to war themselves until at least three months after the completion of arbitration proceedings. Collectively, it was their duty immediately *to sever all commercial, financial and personal relations with any aggressor,* and await the Council's decision on what further action was necessary. This was the application of 'sanctions'. It was clear enough that, if any member of the League were attacked, *all other members* would be expected to come to its aid in this way. Fine words; but would the action match up to them?

The first test came on the 18th September 1931 with the surprise attack of Japanese troops at various points along the South Manchurian Railway, and the subsequent setting-up of the puppet State of 'Manchukuo' in the north-east provinces of China. The motives included the familiar imperialist one, which had led to the earlier contest (1904-5) between Japan and Russia, opposition to communism in both China and Russia, and the diversion of the attention of the Japanese working classes from their existing economic plight by giving them false hopes for the future.

There could be no doubt that this aggression constituted a threat to the 'territorial integrity and existing political independence' of China. In fact the League Assembly declared it to be so after some insistence by the less powerful States; but no attempt was made by any State at all to apply sanctions to Japan. There was a good excuse for this. Great Britain was the only member of the League, besides Japan itself, that could be considered to have much influence in the Far East; for the U.S.A. was not a member. They were all waiting for Britain.

The British attitude soon became apparent. Japan had real grievances, and was setting about rectifying them in the only possible way. China should enter into direct negotiations on the basis of respect for Japan's treaty rights in Manchuria. Why, for heaven's sake? Japan should withdraw on receiving satisfaction for her grievances. Why not immediately? In the meantime, the British would not associate themselves with any action against the Japanese so long as they undertook *to respect British trade interests in China.* So nothing was done.

The second test came in March 1935, when Italian preparations for an attack on Abyssinia were the subject of a formal request by Abyssinia for League intervention. Mussolini's intentions were made perfectly clear in an interview that he gave to a French journalist later on in the same year:

The new Italy needs space for her millions of children, too numerous for her soil; and there, on the high plateaux of Africa, in an immense territory twice as big as France, is one of the last spots in the world that is still free, and where the white race can be acclimatised and find a place to live.[6]

Once again the British attitude was to be decisive; for Britain was the dominant sea power in the Mediterranean, and held the key positions of Gibraltar and Suez. To have stopped the Italian invasion of Abyssinia, which ran into difficulties that were resolved only by the use of mustard gas, would have been relatively easy; but then, Mussolini's fascisti stood in the way of social revolution within Italy itself, and a possible spread of the dreaded communism, by distracting the attention of the poorer classes in the direction of the imagined glories of colonial conquest. Sanctions were not even considered until it was too late. Once again, nothing was done.

After these two fiascos, it is doubtful whether sanctions were considered at all when Hitler embarked on his forward policies – the Rhineland, Austria, Czechoslovakia. All the talk was of 'collective security' by means of alliances; but the only alliance worth having after the fall of Czechoslovakia, namely one with the U.S.S.R. (as events during the war that followed were to show), was avoided – for, after all, was not the communist U.S.S.R. the real enemy? So one with Poland was sought and obtained. In any case, the experience of a quarter of a century before should have made it clear that alliances do not prevent wars, but cause them to spread.

The end of the Second World War brings us, in all essentials, to the brink of the world situation that confronted us until December 1991; and we are faced with the final question: 'Does Tolstoy's philosophy offer any clues to take us back to the turning we have missed?' Certainly nobody else's looks like doing so; and the precipice against which he warned us is now imminent. Surely it would be worth while to spare Tolstoy some thought!

Chapter 17
Towards the precipice

The human race's prospects of survival were considerably better when we were defenceless against tigers than they are today when we have become defenceless against ourselves.
Arnold Toynbee.

HITHERTO we have been considering one by one the main elements of Tolstoy's philosophy, and demonstrating the baselessness of the adverse criticisms that have been levelled against them. Now, however, the time has come to consider the philosophy as a whole, and its relevance to the world of today. It will therefore be convenient to have a summary of it; and what better summary could be found than one couched in Tolstoy's own illuminating style?

Here he deals with the State in its relation to Christianity:

Christianity in its true sense puts an end to the State. It was so understood from its very beginning, and for that Christ was crucified. It has always been so understood by people who were not under the necessity of justifying a Christian State. Only since rulers adopted a nominal external Christianity have men begun to devise all those impossible, cunningly spun theories which pretend to make Christianity compatible with the State. But to every serious and sincere man of our time the incompatibility of true Christianity (the doctrine of humility, forgiveness and love) with the State and its pomp, violence, executions, and wars, is quite obvious. The profession of true Christianity not only excludes the possibility of recognizing the State, but even destroys its foundations.

But if so, and if it is true that Christianity is incompatible with the

State, then the question naturally arises: 'Which is more necessary for the good of humanity, which better secures men's welfare: the political form of life, or its downfall and replacement by Christianity?'.[1]

Elsewhere he connects war and land monopoly:

It would seem clear that during the last century fourteen million people were killed, and that the labour and lives of millions of men are now spent on wars necessary to no one; that the land is mostly in the hands of those who do not work on it, and that the produce of human labour is mostly consumed by those who do not work, and that the deceits which reign in the world exist only because violence is allowed for the sake of suppressing what to some people seems evil, and that we should therefore endeavour to replace violence by persuasion. That this may become possible it is first of all necessary to renounce the right of coercion.[2]

Those to whom persuasion is to be directed are probably not the people who wield power within the State; for, as Tolstoy had discovered experimentally, they are seldom if ever accessible to it – though they may in time repent under the influence of the law of love – but their victims, who, Tolstoy was confident, will one day bring about a new world order, not by violence, but by abstracting themselves from the existing one.

Finally, he puts into a few words the reason usually advanced for the need for the State:

All men in power assert that their authority is necessary to keep bad men from doing violence to the good, thus assuming that they themselves are the good who protect others from the bad.[3]

Where this is leading to is quite obvious; and in fact he goes on to explain that the reason is totally false; for it is the men in power who are themselves the bad men. The review of evidence already presented should suffice to enable the reader to decide whether Tolstoy was right about his own and previous eras. Whether everything is now different – an argument that is sometimes advanced – is something that we must proceed to examine.

At this point there arises a difficulty of scale. A comprehensive account of the world situation at the present time would fill several libraries; and nobody would have either the time or the inclination to read it. Luckily another method is available. Here is a part of the blurb from the dust jacket of the World's Classics edition of Thucydides' *The History of the Peloponnesian War*. It was probably written by the editor, Sir Richard Livingstone, a great advocate of the *practical advantages* of a classical education:

> Thucydides wrote the story of the first democracy in history, and of the fortunes and fall of its empire, but his pages contain the modern world-scene in miniature. Ancient Greece is twentieth-century Europe, incapable of union, tearing itself to pieces in wars which it did not desire but could not avoid. Here are familiar modern phenomena – democracy and imperialism, the class struggle, the revolutionary spirit, the technique of aggression, cynical Real-politik, the importance of sea-power, even quislings and evacuation problems – together with a brilliant account of campaigning in Sicily.

It is possible, in other words, to learn about the problems of modern Europe by studying the history of ancient Greece, because there they are encapsulated in a simpler form. A similar idea pervades modern biology teaching. There is no need to bother with a vast collection of observed facts: students have years ahead of them to collect and assimilate these. If only enough of them are chosen to illustrate undoubted principles, the students will have the best possible start. I shall therefore adopt this method, selecting, as the most apt example for our present purpose, the recent history of the Middle East, the age-old trouble spot of the world, and in particular of Iraq.

Once the scene of the beginnings of two of the earliest known civilisations, those of Sumer and Akkad, Iraq was for centuries until the end of the First World War subject to the domination of the Turks. It was released from that only to fall into the grip of the victorious allies, Britain, France and the United States of America. Its subsequent history, in conjunction with theirs and later on in conjunction also with that of the Union of Soviet Socialist Republics, sums up the major problems whose solution appears to elude the statesmen of the present day. If Tolstoy's philosophy has applications in the Middle East, then it has applications throughout the world.

When the time came after 1918 for the implementation of secret agreements on the fate of the Turkish Empire, the stage was set for disagreements among the allied powers. The British were first to grasp at Middle East oil, having landed troops in Iraq, then known as Mesopotamia, immediately on the outbreak of war with Turkey in 1914. This *fait accompli*, which was probably part of their unacknowledged war aims from the very beginning, was later confirmed with the French and the Russians to the extent that the British were to be allotted control of the two former provinces of Baghdad and Basra; but, not content with these, Lloyd George entered into further negotiations with Clemenceau soon after the armistice, and obtained in addition Mosul, which originally was to have gone to France. In return France was either to receive twenty-five per cent of the oil secured in Iraq by Britain, or, if the development were carried out by a private company, to be allowed to buy twenty-five per cent of the stock.

At this point difficulties were raised by the United States of America, who lodged a stiff protest to the effect that this agreement between Britain and France would 'result in a grave infringement of the mandate principle, which was formulated for the purpose of removing in the future some of the principal causes of international differences'. Strictly speaking, this protest was without legal foundation; for the United States did not belong to the League of Nations, whose members were alone deemed to be competent to formulate the terms of mandates. Curiously enough, Lord Curzon, in his reply, did not take this line, but, reminding the Americans that they already controlled eighty per cent of the oil production of the world, proceeded to tell them that 'the nervousness of American opinion concerning the alleged grasping activities of British oil interests appears singularly unintelligible'. As a result of further complicated negotiations, American companies were nevertheless promised a quarter-interest in the oil of Iraq, and American involvement in the affairs of the Middle East was well and truly under way. The vital importance of oil to modern European civilisation, even at this early date, needs to be constantly borne in mind.

Arguments with the Americans were as nothing compared with the continuing internal problems of Iraq. Arab nationalists had hoped, after their efforts to help the British during the war, for a unified Arab State, or at least for something better than the set of mandates that they actually got. After experimenting with direct rule, and suppressing one revolt by force, the British decided on a compromise. The word 'mandate' was forgotten and replaced by the idea of a treaty of alliance, which Winston Churchill, then Colonial Secretary, promised to see carried out. He had as his principal adviser Colonel T.E. Lawrence, the British link with the Arab uprising of 1916, author of *The Seven Pillars of W isdom,* and known for his sympathy with the Arab cause. In addition, a constitutional monarchy was established, with Amir Faisal, son of the Sharif Hussein who had led the uprising against the Turks, as the first King. The treaty in fact reproduced most of the provisions of the mandate. Iraq promised to respect religious freedom and the rights of foreigners, to treat all provinces equally, and to cooperate with the League of Nations. Britain retained the right to advise on military, judicial and financial affairs. The treaty was signed in 1922, and was intended to last for twenty years.

It lasted for eight. The nationalists considered that the situation it created impeded, not only their political aspirations, but also the economic development of the country. They were probably right: the British would have so arranged matters as to suit British, rather than Iraqi interests. A new treaty was therefore negotiated and signed in 1930. Iraq would be responsible for internal order, and would defend itself against foreign aggression, with British support. Disputes likely to lead to war would be discussed with Britain, and common action would be taken in accordance with the procedures laid down in the Covenant of the League of Nations. The British Army and R.A.F. were to maintain bases near Basra and west of the Euphrates, but, contrary to any normally intelligent person's interpretation of their presence, were not supposed to constitute an occupying force, or an interference with Iraq's sovereign rights.

The period of relative independence that began with the new treaty and Iraq's admission to the League of Nations in 1932 as an independent State was marred by internal dissensions, beginning with an Assyrian uprising in 1933, and continuing with a military *coup d'état* in 1936. The army was henceforth to exercise a decisive influence in politics; but even the army was divided in its loyalties between a faction of older politicians and a group of younger ones who wanted to initiate projects and reforms based on socialism and representative government. Some material progress was in fact made. The Kut al-'Amarah irrigation scheme was completed, and others, to do with oil pipe-lines and railways, to be financed by oil royalties, were begun. The latter method of paying for public works is interesting as a move in the direction of the single tax on the rental value of the resources of nature.

The Second World War brought political differences to a head; and some Arab nationalists in Iraq and elsewhere began secret negotiations with Germany and Italy. The danger became so threatening that British reinforcements were despatched; and a brief contest with the Iraqi forces during May 1941 ended in a British victory and an Iraqi declaration of war on Germany and Italy. This easily settled crisis makes an interesting contrast with what was to follow fifty years later.

The political history of Iraq from 1950 onwards would provide a good detailed case study for the verification of Tolstoy's pronouncements on the subject of violence and the State, were it not for the probability that the reader's state of mind would soon pass from horror to boredom in the face of the damnable iteration of military *coups d'état,* mass executions of defeated rivals and doubtful friends, and reigns of terror backed by the secret police. Saddam Hussein would have ranked as the most successful of the seizers of power, at least in retaining his position by means of the armed force of his Republican Guard, if he had not over-reached himself and gone to war, first with neighbouring Iran (1980-1988), and then in 1991, probably to his surprise and dismay, with the U.S.A. and her allies, over his seizure of the oilfields of Kuwait.

While all this was going on, considerable changes were being made in the administration of Iraq's vast oil reserves. The original agreement between the Iraqi authorities and the Iraq Petroleum Company, which yielded relatively small royalties to the State, was revised in 1952 in favour of one that provided for a fifty/fifty division of receipts after production costs had been met. In other words, the State would collect half the economic rent (Ch.11). Further dissatisfaction in the early 1960's with the State's share in the oil royalties led to Public Law 80, in accordance with which control over all matters connected with oil was transferred to a publicly-owned Iraq National Oil Company, and the granting of concessions to any foreign company was prohibited.

The spending of these oil royalties was partly in the hands of a Development Board, set up in the 1950s, which was responsible for irrigation, flood control, water storage, transportation, and industrial and agricultural expansion. This body incurred much criticism for the attention it gave to long-term projects such as dams and irrigation, bridges and public buildings, while neglecting many short-term ones of more direct use to the population at large. This policy, claimed the critics, was for the benefit mainly of landowners; for the infrastructural investments raised the value of their land. These critics should have followed Henry George and Leo Tolstoy, and pointed out that the introduction of a generalised tax on land values would have siphoned off the economic rent, including that part of it attributable to public works, and made it available, with the oil royalties, for other work of universal benefit. The State's potential income from oil reached a peak in 1973, when, under cover of the fourth Arab-Israeli war, American and Dutch companies were nationalised, as were, two years later, the remaining foreign interests in the Basra Petroleum Company.

By a curious coincidence, the year 1973 saw also a change in the arms trade policies of the 'super-powers', the U.S.A. and the U.S.S.R., both of whom had been willing beforehand to give arms away. The U.S.A. had been anxious to combat world-wide communism, both by assisting régimes of the old persuasion, and by supporting counter-revolutionary movements in countries where communists had gained control. On the other side, the Soviet leaders, while still aiming at an eventual world-wide revolution, had probably also decided that their best chance of future security lay in the Americans' anxiety for their own. These considerations had been sufficient to overcome any motive based on commercial gain.

From 1973 onwards, however, both parties saw things a little differently. The wealthy oil-producing States had begun to charge much more for their oil; so the Americans, whose main customers for arms they were, saw no reason why they should not begin to pay for them. The Russians, on the other hand, were self-sufficient where oil was concerned, but badly needed American dollars to finance their acquisition of western technology. So they began to demand dollars in payment for their arms. From the same period dates the treaty between Iraq and the U.S.S.R., which country, except for the brief period between November 1980, soon after the outbreak of the Iran/ Iraq war, and July 1981, when the Israelis bombed Iraq's nuclear reactor at Osirak, became Iraq's main source of arms.

It must not be imagined that the U.S.A. and the U.S.S.R. were the only suppliers of arms to the Middle East. On the contrary, twenty-four other countries that sold them to both Iran and Iraq during the war of 1980-8 were Austria, Belgium, Brazil, Bulgaria, Chile, China, Czechoslovakia, East Germany, France, West Germany, Greece, Hungary, Italy, North Korea, the Netherlands, Pakistan, Poland, Portugal, South Africa, Spain, Sweden, Switzerland and Yugoslavia. Sixteen more countries supplied arms to either one side or the other. In view of all this, what are we to make of the repeated appeals for a cease-fire issued by the United Nations Organisation? No whole can be better than its parts. Britain supplied both sides, claiming that only 'non-lethal' equipment was being sold. Here is the official excuse for selling any at all. It comes from a

Ministry of Defence letter dated the 17th May 1982 and quoted in a Campaign Against Arms Trade publication:

> Our policy is one of neutrality in the conflict between Iran and Iraq. ... We are prepared to consider requests for the supply of defence equipment from either side on a case by case basis, taking into account our neutrality obligations, our relations with the countries concerned, and the need to work for a peaceful solution to the conflict.[4]

One can easily imagine Tolstoy's scornful denunciation of the miserable euphemism 'defence', and a sarcastic enquiry about how it was imagined that a supply of ancillary equipment for murder could contribute to any 'peaceful solution'.

We have laid great stress on the open and violent seizures of power, and wrong-doing while in power, of the various Iraqi administrations; but further consideration needs to be given to the actions of those others who had helped to supply the armaments without which the Iraqis and their enemies would have had to live comparatively blameless lives. Take for example the British Cabinet. True, it was not put in its place by a military *coup d'état,* but by means of a procedure of election that is commonly described as 'democratic' (i.e. pertaining to rule by the people). A little consideration, however, of party finance, of how candidates are chosen *before* an election, and of periodic revelations of consultancy fees paid to Ministers and M.P.s by organisations with axes to grind, should convince thinking people that their own part in the conduct of public affairs is negligible. The success of 'genial humbug' (Ch.5), in fact, makes the use of force unnecessary. Furthermore, British administrations, particularly in their early days, are able to act in a manner that would run contrary to the inclinations of a large majority of the electorate. Permitting the sale of military equipment, even 'non-lethal', to both sides in the Iran/Iraq war is a case in point.

But they did more than permit it: they gave it positive encouragement. In 1983, for example, when Iraq's failing oil revenues began to cause payment problems, they came to the rescue by arranging for a £250m. loan to Iraq by the merchant bankers Morgan Grenfell to be backed by the Export Credits Guarantee Department (E.C.G.D.). It would be backed, in other words, by the British taxpayer. Further such credits were arranged in 1988 (£340m.) and 1989 (£250m). This sudden drop was caused not only by the arrest of the *Observer* reporter Farzad Bazoft by the Iraqi authorities on a trumped-up charge of spying, and that of the British nurse Daphne Parish for having given him a lift in her car, but also by the fact that Iraqi repayments were nearly £80m. in arrears.

These export credits were the subject of further questions in both Houses of Parliament. In the House of Lords a member wanted to know, in 1989, why it was that the administration was willing, despite that country's deplorable record in the matter of human rights, to continue to run considerable financial risks in guaranteeing its payments. Lord Trefgarne, Trade Minister, replied as follows:

'If we cut off our trading relations ... we would lose many opportunities to convey our views on other matters'.

Then, after asserting that trade sanctions – with which the question had nothing to do – had never worked, he went on to say:

'Iraq is sitting on oil reserves second only to those of Saudi Arabia. Indeed, I think that that makes it the second largest possessor of oil reserves in the world'.[5]

What kind of an official scale of values do such replies reveal?

The dangerous situation thus created by Saddam Hussein and his foreign arms suppliers came to a head on the 2nd August 1990, when Iraq, having at that time an army 955,000 strong, 5,500 tanks and 689 combat aircraft, marched into neighbouring Kuwait, where the army numbered 20,300, tanks 245 and combat aircraft 35. An unsatisfactory boundary was alleged; but the real reason was that Kuwait's oil reserves amounted to 97.1 billion barrels, not far short of Iraq's own 100 billion barrels. The eight-year war with Iran had left Iraq short of ready money. Kuwait, in contrast to nationalist and socialist Iraq, had retained the original social structure left by the allies after the First World War, namely government by large landowners. This structure had been maintained, not by arms and repression, but by one of the world's most complete welfare systems for its citizens, and the importation of many foreign workers (60 per cent of the total) for the least pleasant occupations. Neither system can be guaranteed to last.

Both, in fact, found themselves in the melting-pot during the early part of 1991. Saddam Hussein failed to meet the deadline imposed by the Security Council for his withdrawal from Kuwait; and the 15th January 1991 passed by with no promise from him but that any attempt to remove him would result in a 'blood-bath'. It did. George Bush, President of the U.S.A., gave the word for military action to 'liberate Kuwait'; and six weeks ensued of the most intense and horrific aerial bombardment short of the nuclear that the world had ever seen. After this the land war was over within a week. Casualties on the allied side did not exceed three figures; but it has been estimated that the number of Iraqis killed or wounded ran into hundreds of thousands.

A lenient verdict on this catastrophic chain of events involving Iraq would be one of total irresponsibility on the part of all the States involved. Tolstoy would have gone further, and pronounced them guilty of robbery and murder.

The example of Iraq has been selected because it is typical. Study of any serious newspaper over a period of time will confirm this. All over the world, local landed *élites* in the former subject countries arrange to satisfy the special requirements of 'developed' countries in the way of either mineral deposits, as in the case of Iraq, or of consumer goods such as coffee, rice, tea, soya beans and spices, unsuitable for growing in a northern climate. They are thus enabled to buy the products of industrial countries, notably armaments, with which they proceed to keep their mainly landless populations in a state of subjugation, and, according to perceived needs, to set one oppressed people to fight against another.

The 'developed' countries in their turn still feel the pressure to export by reason of astronomical differences in wealth, caused by gross maldistribution of land. Too few working people receive as monetary wages anything approaching the natural level, namely an equivalent to the value they have added to the products they help to make; and they are therefore unable to buy as much as they have produced. Production so rendered apparently surplus to general needs at home will then take the form, either of luxury articles for the rich, or of goods saleable abroad, including those same armaments, the trade in which, as we have seen, the State is willing to assist at the taxpayers' expense.

The remedy of the single tax, as prescribed by George and Tolstoy, goes to the heart of this dangerous situation. Applied in the 'developed' countries, it would enable wages to rise to their natural level as just defined, increase the effective demand for goods in general use, and eliminate the most urgent motive for exporting. Applied in the 'developing' countries, it would, for the first time since the onset of the colonising drive, make it necessary for agricultural land to be put to its most productive use per unit of area, instead of per person employed. Cash crops for export, as favoured by the owners of vast estates, would gradually by replaced, as in California from 1887 onwards (Ch.15), by more varied, labour-intensive and smaller-scale cultivation favouring the people at large. With the *élites* would disappear the need for arms.

Mineral deposits, as for example the oil in Iraq, are a special case. In all other instances, the proceeds of the single tax would be for local spending; but, if conflict is to be avoided, royalties from mining and oil drilling need to be distributed world-wide. After all, the United Nations Organisation has declared the minerals on the deep-sea bed to be the 'common heritage of mankind'. Why not the dry-land ones?

The case history that has just been set out in detail should be a sufficient demonstration of the deadly danger that could now be very close. What needs to be steadily borne in mind in the face of it is the progression of events that has brought us into our present predicament: land monopoly – poverty – huge

States with insufficient popular control – territorial and trade wars – imperialism – post-imperialism – administrations ruled by monopoly interests, the most immediately dangerous of which is the arms industry. The situation as Tolstoy described it has worsened; but the remedies he proposed still cry out for a fair trial.

Chapter 18
Tolstoy and *perestroika*

A new science of politics is needed for a new world.
Alexis de Tocqueville.

THE international aspect of the world malaise and how it may be cured is illustrated very well by the case history of Iraq; but, when it comes to considering the application of the Tolstoyan philosophy on a national scale – for national events both precede and determine international ones – no study will suffice but that of a 'super-power', where economic injustice, irresponsible arbitrary government and geographical extent have reached their furthest yet known limits. In other words, the type of State to be considered is one where Tolstoy's criticisms are most relevant.

A brief survey of Russian history (Ch.5) has already made it clear enough that there at least the State was both founded on conquest and exploitation, and subsequently shaped for their maintenance. Not only this, but the cold reception accorded to Tolstoy's apparently modest proposal for land reform, taken in conjunction with the repressive measures he encountered for use in asserting the predominance of the great landowners, and for guarding against revolt (Ch.6), are obvious signs that the nature of the Russian State in his time was the same as ever. It had been established by landowners for landowners; and Tolstoy's 'apparently modest proposal' was in fact a proposal that it should abandon its first and principal function.

The U.S.S.R. (1917-1991), where the old tyranny of landownership was replaced by one of party bosses, qualifies for our purpose on the grounds of both economic injustice and irresponsible and arbitrary government; for the *élite,* as we shall see, prospered greatly, while more than half the population remained miserably poor. Its size is important also, because, whatever mode of economic exploitation is adopted, be it land monopoly, dictatorship, slavery, tariff barriers to enable home customers to be charged artificially high prices for their goods, or whatever else, the biggest gains are to be expected in the biggest countries. Not only this, but in the biggest countries the machinery of State is most remote, and most likely to be regarded as permanent and untouchable.

The U.S.A. also may be considered to be a suitable candidate on the grounds of size, economic injustice, and government against the common interest, concealed though it may be behind the same 'genial humbug' that prevails in Britain. Now the tentative efforts being made there (Ch.15) on behalf of what has been shown to be the fundamental and essential economic reform are highly laudable in themselves; but it would take a brave man to assert that the idea is going to spread in anything like the way a forest fire spreads, of its own accord. The Federal administration has yet to be convinced of its necessity; but then the Federal administration of the U.S.A., like the old administration of the Russian Empire, exists to further the purposes of the exploiters. Those who think that this is an exaggeration should read A.J. Nock's convenient summary[1] of how exploitative institutions were transferred from Britain to the American colonies, and how the Federal constitution was imposed by fraud on the original States after Independence. They should then consider the reason for the war of 1861-65, which was not the abolition of slavery as is popularly supposed, but the preservation of the Union. So far there have been no more such splits in this monolithic structure, nor are there signs of any impending.

Matters are far otherwise in the former U.S.S.R., where not only have the bonds of union been cut, but also the familiar style of authoritarian rule by Communist Party bosses is at an end. There are even some grounds for hope that the principle of the single tax may eventually come to be understood and implemented, before the idea occurs to enough power-lovers that a return to pre-revolutionary conditions might be in their interest. Of these grounds the principal one is that, for about seventy years, or nearly three generations, there has been no private ownership of land. How fitting it would be if this vital part of the Tolstoyan philosophy should receive its first full implementation in his own country! Let us then examine our reasons for thinking that this is still possible.

In order to appreciate the scope and significance of the changes in progress, it is necessary first to form a general impression of how exploitation was achieved under one-party government in the unreformed socialist State. Our witnesses are Mikhail Gorbachev, former President of the Soviet Union, and Konstantin Simis, a barrister forced to emigrate from it on account of his too enthusiastic defence of political offenders. Let Gorbachev have the first word:

> Many Party organizations in the regions were unable to uphold principles or to attack with determination bad tendencies, slack attitudes, the practice of covering up for one another and lax discipline. More often than not, the principles of equality among Party members were violated. Many Party members in leading posts stood beyond control and criticism, which led to failures in work and to serious malpractices.
>
> At some administrative levels there emerged a disrespect for the law and encouragement of eyewash and bribery, servility and glorification. Working people were justly indignant at the behavior of people who, enjoying trust and responsibility, abused power, suppressed criticism, *made fortunes* and, in some cases, even became accomplices in – if not organizers of – criminal acts.[2]

Simis' description of the way of life of the ruling *élite* is one of people living in a world apart. Their housing, naturally of superior quality, was, he wrote, isolated from that of the common people. Their salaries could be as much as thirty times the official minimum, which the average for manual and office workers failed even to equal. Their salaries, moreover, were no measure of their actual standard of living; for their needs were catered for in the Kremlin stores, inaccessible to others; and much of their purchasing was done with vouchers, paid for at about one-third of their face value. As if all this were not enough, they were entitled to fringe benefits on an ascending scale according to rank, culminating, for members of the *Politburo,* in country palaces, lavishly staffed, equipped and provisioned free of charge.

Since an official would lose all this if he were to lose his post, there was a standing temptation to use the post for the acquisition of the private and unassailable fortune hinted at by Gorbachev. Here is an extreme example from Simis:

> For several years, agents of Shevarnadze's [sic] Ministry for Internal Affairs shadowed all the leading functionaries in the Party and state *apparat* of Georgia, as well as their families, and much compromising evidence was gathered. For instance, the trade in the highest posts in the Party and state *apparat* had become so blatant that an underground millionaire, Babunashvili, was able to order for himself the post of Minister of Light Industry. Babunashvili headed an illegal company which produced and marketed fabrics, but his ambition was satisfied neither by his multi-million-ruble income nor by his business activities, and he decided that he wanted to cap his career by combining in himself both sides of Soviet organized crime: by being the corrupter (underground business) and the corrupted (government).[3]

It does not take much imagination to see that there is here alone the potential for considerable resistance to any attempt at reform. But resistance from these quarters would be negligible compared with that to be expected from what has come to be known as the military-industrial complex. Professor B.P. Pockney of the University of Surrey, has given an estimate of its size and power.[4]

The complex comprised over fourteen industrial ministries, which produced consumer goods as well as armaments. For example, the tools that made sprinklers for agricultural machines also made parts for bombers. The military budget for 1991, despite the beginnings of *perestroika* or 'reconstruction', rose to 94 billion roubles; but this did not include some elements of civilian budgets that were going to be devoted to military uses. For example, part of the budget for the Ministry of Railways was to be spent on transporting troops. As a result, somewhere between 20 and 45 per cent of the national budget was for military purposes. It must also be taken into account that there were between 5 and 5.5 million men in the Red Army and the K.G.B., and that the uniformed forces were supported by somewhere between 20 and 50 million civilian workers. The U.S.S.R.'s total labour force amounted to only 120 million people. The Soviet economy, in other words, was on a permanent war footing, with all that this phrase of poignant memory implied for the living standards of the population at large. Those readers who feel inclined to doubt Professor Pockney's summing-up will find it amply confirmed in a book by Eduard Shevardnadze,[5] well-known as a former liberal-minded Foreign Minister.

What was it that made possible an effort on this gigantic scale? It was of course the very size of the Soviet Union. If each constituent Republic had been responsible for collecting and spending its own revenue, none of this would have happened. Such a situation may have represented the limit of the Republics' ambitions before the dissolution of the Union; but a single step in this direction would have been enough to sound the alarm bells within the military-industrial complex and the armed forces themselves. Resistance to *perestroika* from these quarters would have been caused, not so much by any change in the economic system, or extension of the political rights of the individual citizen, as by the threat to the Union posed by a new federal treaty that extended the rights of the Republics.

So far we have been dealing with the relative certainties of a static and observable situation; but, when we come to think about *perestroika,* attempts to implement it, and the reactions that it provoked, we are faced with the incoherence that is a characteristic of all revolutions. Even at the best of times, politicians deal in vague generalities, in order that their statements may bear the interpretations that different sets of people may choose to put upon them, or provide an escape route in case of future difficulties. In the midst of the turmoil of revolution, they will go a step further, and perform a balancing act, saying one thing one day and saying or doing its opposite the next. In this way they hope to confuse the opposition and keep a secure hold on their office.

All this makes difficulties enough where a State with one central administration is concerned; but, in the former Soviet Union, things have been made far more complicated by the competition of the administrations of the fifteen Republics, all with their special axes to grind. Perhaps in fifty years time, when historians have had a chance to get to work on all the records and memoirs, it will be possible for a connected tale to be told. In the meantime, the impression given by events is one of unmitigated chaos, of which one must make the best one can.

What, first of all, was this *perestroika,* about which so much has been said and written? According to Gorbachev himself,[6] and in very general terms, it involved primarily the improvement of the economic situation by the granting of independence and powers of self-financing to hitherto officially controlled enterprises. This was the beginning of the 'market economy'. Then there was more *glasnost* or 'openness', coupled with greater involvement of the workers themselves in the production process. In the social sphere, it meant more popular participation in government, and increased concern for 'the culture of every individual and society as a whole'.

The switch from single-party dictatorship to freely-elected representative government, commonly known inaccurately as 'democracy', began in June 1988, when Gorbachev, presiding over a conference of the Communist Party of the Soviet Union (C.P.S.U.), proposed measures that involved a movement of executive authority away from party officials and towards elected deputies of Soviets (councils) at all levels of society. At the highest level there was to be a Soviet Congress. The conference approved the measures; and, in March 1989, there was a gratifyingly large turn-out for the first genuine parliamentary elections to be held in the Soviet Union since 1917. Gorbachev himself was elected a few weeks later to be executive President of the new Soviet Congress.

Gorbachev's statement of the aims of *perestroika* contains no treatment at length of that controversial subject, the tenure of land; but, when he comes to the question of agriculture, there is a passing indication of his opinion that rent should go into the public revenue:

> Today, we have large collective farms and sovkhozes [state farms] in many agricultural areas. Large work teams, sections and complexes have been organized. They are somewhat divorced from the land, and this affects end results. Today, we must ensure a more solid and direct connection with the interests of the individual through collective, family and *rental contracts* within the framework of these collective and state farms. Then we will combine the advantages of a large collective economy with the individual's interests. This is exactly what we need. If we act in this way we can make impressive strides in solving the problem of foodstuffs within two or three years.[7]

Practice to date does not appear to have come up to his expectations; for there is evidently a widespread belief, encouraged by western politicians, that the private ownership of land is an essential element in the market economy. Private ownership of agricultural land has in fact been allowed in accordance with a law passed in December 1990 by the Congress of Russian People's Deputies; but it is ownership that is subject to restrictions. The buyer may not sell at all within ten years; and, when the ten years are up, he may sell it only to the local Soviet, or council.

This measure, which in no way satisfies Henry George's and Leo Tolstoy's principle that economic rent is the only just source of public revenue, was greeted with enthusiasm by both traditionalists and reformers; and Boris Yeltsin, President of the Russian Republic, described it as 'historic'. Mikhail Gorbachev, on the other hand, as we should have expected from the piece of writing just quoted, had expressed, firmly but unavailingly, his opposition to any form of private land ownership whatsoever. Now his demand for a nationwide referendum on the subject will obviously not be satisfied.

A further threat on similar lines has become apparent in the disorderly fashion in which the transfer of public property to private ownership has been taking place. Luxurious country homes, for example, have been sold to senior officials at bargain prices, presumably land and all. If the buildings alone were sold, and the land leased out, there would be no cause for alarm; but, otherwise, the first steps towards a return to pre-1917 conditions have been taken. Gorbachev did his best to halt them by means of a presidential decree of the 12th August 1991, setting up a central agency, *Soyuzgosfond,* to regulate the terms of such transfers and negotiate property claims with the Republics. This work, to be effective, needed to be done according to sound Georgist and Tolstoyan principles.

If there is anything that can still be done to stave off the worst effects of the private ownership of land, it will not remain undone for lack of expert outside advice. Around the turn of 1990-1991, an open letter was sent to Gorbachev, signed by thirty-one eminent economists, explaining in detail why and how the land of the U.S.S.R. should be retained in public ownership, and public revenue raised by the charging of rent for the use of it. Three of them – Franco Modigliani, Robert Solow and James Tobin – are Nobel prize-winners.[8]

Later on, in May 1991, an American team of four visited the U.S.S.R. with the same end in view. They were George Collins, Director of the Henry George School of New York; Dr Steven Cord, whose efforts have been mainly responsible for the startling successes of the two-rate local property tax in Pennsylvania (Ch.15); Ted Gwartney, professional valuer in California; and Professor Nicolaus Tideman, who has worked hard to establish contacts with politicians, civil servants and university economists in Eastern Europe. These men made it clear that, apart from the general advantages of the single tax, a special one in the former U.S.S.R., (now to be known as the Commonwelath of Independent States) would be to stop the notorious waste of natural resources engendered by the practice over many years of allowing their use free of charge, and raising public revenue in other ways.

The outcome of the contest determining who would have responsibility,for collecting and distributing revenue could have been seen in fairly simple terms as a personal one between

Gorbachev, who remained in favour of keeping as much as possible of the power centrally, and Yeltsin, who preferred to press on with giving effect to republican autonomy. From one point of view, it was to be hoped that Gorbachev would retain whatever power he had left long enough to give land value taxation a start throughout the Soviet Union. There would then have been an analogy with Tolstoy's wish (Ch.12) that the Tsar would use his despotic authority to introduce it, and then abdicate. On the other hand, Tolstoy would also have been pleased to see the dissolution of the latest version of the Russian Empire. In the event, the second satisfaction would have been gained at the expense of the first. The signs (in 1992) now point to the establishment of republican autonomy within a loose commonwealth, or perhaps in the end two, one Slav and one Muslim.

Gorbachev's situation at the beginning of 1991 being what it was, it is hardly surprising that, when he delivered his televised New Year's address, he should have shown some weariness in making the following admission:

> 1990 has been a year of difficult and important decisions – about ownership, power and land.[10]

Worse was to follow on the afternoon of Sunday the 18th August, when a group of eight emissaries from Moscow called on him at his holiday home in the Crimea to announce that there had been a *coup d'état,* and that he had been deposed and was under house-arrest.

The main instigators of the *coup* were Yazov, representing the army; Kryuchkov of the K.G.B.; Pugo of the Ministry of the Interior; Pavlov, Prime Minister and head of the bureaucracy; Baklanov of the military-industrial complex; Tizyakov of the immense state industries; 'farmer' Starodubtsev; and Gennadi Yanayev, representing no vested interest in particular, but chosen as a figure-head simply because Gorbachev had been ill-advised enough to choose him as his Vice-President. Otherwise, it was a representative collection of men attached to those very organisations that have already been pointed out as under particular threat from the reformers. They miscalculated in two important respects.

In the first place, they had no attractive alternative to the future towards which the reforms were tending, but only a vague idea of returning to the familiar conditions of the past, which had suited them well enough, but left the majority out in the cold. As Gorbachev himself warned his captors: 'Look ahead', he said, 'look two, three, four steps ahead'. They had done nothing of the kind, and as a consequence had no conception of the popular opposition they were likely to encounter.

The shrewd Boris Yeltsin arrived at a juster estimate of the temper of his countrymen. Learning of the movement of hundreds of tanks in the direction of the massively-constructed White House, headquarters of the new Russian Parliament, he decided on resistance. A crowd of about 200,000 gathered to protect the threatened symbol of the new order, and up went the barricades. Yeltsin himself, with his confident bearing and a voice that needed help from no loud-hailer, called on the military not to fire on their own people. This was where the junta had made their second miscalculation. Did they think they could carry out a repetition of the massacre at the Winter Palace in 1905?

Three young men were killed, more by accident than design, and became in the process Heroes of the Soviet Union; but senior army officers decided to obey Yeltsin rather than the junta, and began to withdraw their troops from the city. It was the beginning of the end. On Wednesday the 21st August, Kryuchkov telephoned one of Yeltsin's aides to tell him that there would be no attack; and a delegation was soon on its way to bring Gorbachev back from the Crimea.

In the long run, this personal triumph on the part of Yeltsin increased the strength of his political position, and enabled him to proceed with an economic revolution running contrary to Gorbachev's known wishes. On the 28th October 1991, in the course of a long speech to the Republic's Congress, in which he outlined a 'a daring reform programme', he made the following pronouncement:

The President will also submit to parliament a package of amendments to the land reform law, to strengthen the legal basis for change in this area, and at last to permit the purchase and sale of land.[11]

This statement would seem on the face of it to refer to the sale of the freehold of land, as it is understood in non-communist countries; but Russian visitors to England have explained that it is rather the sale of the *leasehold* that was in question. Everything therefore depended on the amount of rent initially collected by the State, and on whether the terms of the leases included one for its regular revision. If they did not, then an ever-increasing proportion of the economic rent (Ch.11) would be lost to the public revenue.

A second visit to Russia by Steven Cord and a party of seven in October 1991 confirmed the statement of the Russians in England, but made it clear that the rent (or, for non-rent-payers, the land value tax) was to be at a very low level, sufficient only to finance improvement to the land, together with associated activities. It is a fair assumption that sale prices will be correspondingly high. It is also clear that the question of revised assessments has not yet been tackled, except in the vaguest possible terms:

Bids for land rent are reviewed according to changes in improvement conditions independent of land users.[12]

The consequence of the unsuccessful *coup* was Gorbachev's resignation as General Secretary of the C.P.S.U., the confiscation of all its property, and the banning of its activities in the armed forces, the K.G.B. and all other law enforcement agencies. Seventy-four years of one-party rule came thereby to a decisive end. Even more significantly, at 5 p.m. on Thursday the 12th December 1991 the Union itself was dissolved, and Gorbachev made effectively redundant. Not surprisingly, before general dissolution had been contemplated, among the first Republics to secede had been the the Baltic countries of Esthonia, Latvia and Lithuania; but none of these has the economic importance of the seceding Ukraine, the Union's granary. The problem of this and other such specially endowed Republics calls for a solution in the way of a sharing of economic rent between the members of the commonwealth or commonwealths that emerge from the chaos.

Though the dissolution of the Union would certainly have struck Tolstoy as a step in the right direction, it would hardly have gone any way at all to satisfy his ideal of individual self-sufficiency. But then, such an ideal is not to be taken too seriously; for Man is, and always has been a social animal. His social needs probably found adequate expression in the ancient Russian system of peasant local government (Ch.8), which was withdrawn from the jurisdiction of the landowners at the time of the abolition of serfdom (1861). Its components were the *mir* and the *volost*. The first was an assembly of all the householders in a village, and the second an assembly of representatives from a group of villages, or canton. They both had judicial and administrative functions. As has already been suggested, Tolstoy must have been aware of all this; and the indications are that he did not disapprove of it.

The *mir*, like the Anglo-Saxon 'folk-moot', is the democratic ideal whereby all citizens have a voice in making decisions that affect the common interest. Would that the process of fragmenting government could be carried thus far! In any case, revenue-raising needs to be carried out at the lowest possible level, if it is not eventually to be withdrawn from the reach of popular control, and to become an instrument of exploitation. Where it *has* been subject to popular control, as in New Zealand (Ch.15), it will be remembered that practical common sense dictated its derivation from economic rent.

Unfortunately, the Western advisers to Yeltsin's first administration had other ideas.

In the debate about the fate of land – and the liberty of the citizen – it comes as no surprise to learn that the Russians came to realise the significance of Tolstoy's philosophy for their future. Ironically, this new appreciation was first disclosed by Moscow's last hardline Communist Party leader, Ivan Polozkov, in a protest against the Russian parliament's decision to allow peasants to own land. He cited one of the letters written by Tolstoy to Pyotr Stolypin, the tsar's prime minister who sought to privatise common land – a policy that Tolstoy characterised as a "swinish trick".[13]

At first, there was strong sympathy for the Tolstoyan strategy from Boris Yeltsin. He wanted to develop a strategy that enabled peasants to possess land, with the State retaining the freehold. This attitude was articulated after the announcement of a compromise embodied in a law in December 1990. Yeltsin was challenged by an American reporter, who asked whether the restrictions on land ownership were in the spirit of freedom. That was when Yeltsin replied:

> You don't understand the Russian spirit. People here do not understand the concept of buying and selling land. The land is like a mother. You don't sell your mother.[14]

But something significant was to happen, between the expression of this view and the stormy Congress of People's Deputies in April 1992, which was to transform Yeltsin's outlook. A constitutional crisis exploded when the conservatives obstructed Yeltsin's proposal that land, after all, ought to be privatised. On April 17, by a majority of 478 to 380, conservative deputies blocked the discussion of a constitutional amendment which would have permitted the purchase and sale of land. In his closing address, the president admonished the deputies for failing to pass that law.[15]

What had happened to change Yeltsin's mind about the ownership of mother earth? Money: the need to accommodate western perceptions of what constituted the elements of the market economy, in return for the aid that Russia needed.[16] Yeltsin was rewarded a few days after his censorious criticism of the deputies, when multi-billion dollar loans were made available to him at the IMF's meeting in Washington, DC, on April 27.

That three Nobel prize-winning economists should join their colleagues to commend what was the Tolstoy/George model of private possession aligned with social ownership of land and rental revenue, ought, one would have thought, to have at least attracted a reappraisal of orthodox economic attitudes. Instead, some of the experts went so far as to want to disallow a review of their prescriptions. Consider, for example, how the Georgist plan – a general tax on land rents, offset by a reduction in the tax burden on other forms of income – would attract private foreign investment into Russia (which would reduce the dependence on IMF/World Bank loans), and would speed reindustrialisation along market lines.[17] Such a strategy would be viewed with horror by those who wish to intimidate governments into emulating a seriously imperfect system:

> The need to attract additional capital from abroad will require that countries in transition build into their tax systems appropriate incentives to speed up this process. It would be harmful and inadmissible, however, to initiate unfair tax competition among the countries in transition, or to transform them into tax havens, or for them to become a bridge for various forms of tax evasion on an international scale.[18]

Why? There is nothing in international law which says that every country should suffer from a uniformity of tax-induced misery. There is no reason why Russia should not finally correct the error of Tsar Nicholas (the error which ultimately permitted the Red revolution), and carry out rational reforms that would ensure social justice and economic freedom outside the framework of bureaucratic controls. The objective conditions exist in Russia which make the Georgist/Tolstoyan economic programme realistic. In the West, resistance to a land-tax led strategy of social transformation relies on the argument that land is privately owned, and therefore ought not to be singled out for special taxation. The dubious moral merits of that argument need not detain us, for they do not apply in Russia, where the Federation owns all the land and natural resources. Russia could therefore revert to the time-honoured principles employed by mankind, based on social ownership and individual possession. This sophisticated approach to property rights would enable people to possess as much land as they could use, in return for the payment of rent to the community for the privilege (that rental income, of course, would be shared equally by everyone through the public purse). This one bold principle would correct the structural flaw in the market model, eliminating the instability and unfairness which has characterised that system for two centuries.

This strategy is even now attainable in Russia, for on December 27, 1991, President Yeltsin signed a decree on taxation which stated, in Article 21 (b), that a land tax should be instituted. Modifications to the philosophy behind this tax are necessary, however, for it is cast as a local revenue-raiser. It ought to be a federally-administered macro-economic tool for efficiency and social justice. Appropriately structured, and linked to a sophisticated philosophy on land tenure, the land-value tax would release Russia once and for all from the constraints on the energies of people who wish for no more than the freedom to work for a decent life for themselves and their families.

We now give a final emphasis to what Tolstoy put first among the elements of his philosophy, namely the moral code enunciated in the 'Sermon on the Mount'. He did so because he felt that the future of the world depended above all on *metanoia,* or change of heart in each individual person. Perhaps in the end he will be proved to have been right; but that is not a good enough reason for an individual's failure, here and now, to make every effort to achieve a good mental grasp of how exploiters, by any means whatsoever, use the State as a tool to further their own ends. Knowledge is as immediately important to the world as a desire for a clear conscience. This Tolstoy provided in good measure.

It is as well to remember, though we have been thinking primarily about Christianity, that there are other religions, and among them those that teach the same morality as Jesus of Nazareth. One has only to think of the following:

Do not approve for another what you do not like for yourself.
Gospel of Zarathustra.

Will ye tell others to be righteous and not practise righteousness yourself? *The Koran, 2,44.*

Return love for hatred. *The Tao Te Ching.*

Hatred is never diminished by hatred. Hatred is diminished by love. This is the eternal law. *The Dhammapada (Buddhist).*

O God, it is Thy word that mankind is a single nation, so all human beings are born free and equal in dignity and rights, they are endowed with love and conscience and should act towards one another in the spirit of brotherhood. *The Koran.*

If there be righteousness in the heart,
There will be beauty in the character.
If there is beauty in the character,
There will be harmony in the home.
If there be harmony in the home,
There will be order in the nation.
When there is order in each nation,
There will be peace in the world. *Chinese proverb.*

Is there not here the basis for the teaching of a comparative religion, transcending all divisive dogma and mystery, that will unite all those, of whatever race or culture, who desire the future well-being and tranquillity of mankind? Tolstoy himself evidently thought so; for he went to considerable pains to compile a large collection of such extracts, which he thought of as the Bible of an already existing universal faith. It has been published in Russian under the titles of *A Circle of Reading, For Every Day* and *Sayings of the wise.*

All in all, surely mankind has at last had enough bitter experience of the false pathways that have already been mapped and followed so often? So can we hope that the people themselves, at this crucial time, with the Nation/State showing signs of terminal decline, with socialism in disarray, land-and-capital monopoly heading more rapidly than ever for the rocks, and religious intolerance still poisoning human relationships,

will give serious study to Tolstoy's message – and take pause?
*There is nothing so powerful as a set of ideas whose time has
come.*

Appendix 1

To the Emperor Nicholas II. Gaspra, 28 January 1902.

Dear Brother,

I consider this form of address to be most appropriate because I address you in this letter not so much as a tsar but as a man – a brother – and furthermore because I am writing to you as it were from the next world, since I expect to die very soon.

I did not want to die without telling you what I think of your present activity, of what it could be, of what great good it could bring to millions of people and to yourself, and of what great evil it can bring to those people and yourself if it continues in the same direction in which it is now going.

A third of Russia is in a state of emergency, i.e. is outside the law. The army of police – open and secret – is constantly growing. Over and above the hundreds of thousands of criminals, the prisons, places of exile, and labour camps are overflowing with political prisoners, to whom workers are now being added as well. The censorship has descended to nonsensical prohibitions, which it never descended to in the worst period of the '40s. Religious persecutions were never so frequent and cruel as they are now, and they are becoming more and more cruel and frequent. Armed forces are concentrated everywhere in the cities and industrial centres and are sent out against the people with live cartridges. In many places there has already been bloodshed between brothers, and further and more cruel bloodshed is imminent everywhere and will inevitably follow.

And as a result of all this intense and cruel activity on the part of the government, the people who work on the land – those 100 million people on whom the power of Russia is based – despite the excessive growth of the state budget or, more likely, because of this growth, become more impoverished every year, so that famine has become a normal occurrence. And general discontent with the government among all classes and a hostile attitude towards it has become just as normal an occurrence.

There is one cause of all this and it is manifestly evident: namely that your aides assure you that by halting any movement of life among the people they are thereby assuring the well-being of the people and your own peace and security. But one can far more easily halt a river's flow than halt mankind's continual progress forward as ordained by God. It is understandable that the people to whom the present order of things is advantageous and who in the depth of their souls say 'aprks nous le daluge', can and must assure you of this; but it is amazing that you, a free man not lacking for anything, and a reasonable and good man, can believe them and follow their terrible advice to do or allow to be done so much evil for the sake of such an impracticable purpose as halting the eternal movement of mankind from evil to goodness, from darkness to light.

Surely you cannot fail to know that as long as we have been aware of human life, the forms of this life, economic and social as well as religious and political, have constantly changed, progressing from harsh, cruel and unreasonable forms to more gentle, humane and reasonable ones.

Your advisers tell you that this is not true, that just as Orthodoxy and autocracy were once natural to the Russian people, so they are natural to them now and will be natural to them to the end of time, and that therefore for the good of the Russian people it is necessary at all costs to maintain these two interconnected forms: religious belief and the political system. But this is really a double falsehood. Firstly, it is quite impossible to say that Orthodoxy, which was once natural to the Russian people, is natural to them now. You can see from the reports of the Over-Procurator of the Synod that the most spiritually developed of the people, despite all the disadvantages and dangers which they are subject to in renouncing Orthodoxy, are going over in greater and greater numbers to the so-called sects. Secondly, if it is true that Orthodoxy is natural to the people, then there is no reason to maintain this form of faith so forcibly and to persecute those who reject it with such cruelty.

As for autocracy – then similarly if it was natural to the Russian people when that people still believed that the tsar was an infallible God on earth and that he governed the people by himself, it is far from natural to them now that everyone knows, or as soon as they acquire a bit of education find out, that firstly, a good tsar is only 'un heureux hasard' and that tsars can be and have been monsters and idiots, like Ivan IV or Paul, and secondly, that however good a tsar may be, he simply cannot govern 130 million people by himself, and the people are governed by the tsar's closest advisers, who are more concerned about their own position than about the good of the people. You will say: a tsar can select as his aides people who are disinterested and good. Unfortunately a tsar cannot do this because he knows only a few dozen people who are close to him by accident or as a result of various intrigues, and who diligently fend away from him all those who might replace them. So the tsar does not choose from among those thousands of vital, energetic, genuinely enlightened, honest people who have the social cause at heart, but only from among those about whom Beaumarchais said: 'médiocre et rampant et on parvient á tout'[1]. And if many Russian people are prepared to obey the tsar, they cannot without a feeling of outrage obey people of their own circle whom they despise and who so often govern the people in the name of the tsar.

You have probably been deceived about the people's love for autocracy and its representative, the tsar, by the fact that everywhere in Moscow and in other cities where you appear, crowds of people run after you with shouts of 'Hurrah!' Don't believe that this is an expression of devotion to you – they are crowds of inquisitive people who would run just the same after any unusual spectacle. Often these people whom you take to be expressing their love for you are nothing more than a crowd gathered together and organised by the police and obliged to represent themselves as your devoted people, as happened, for example, with your grandfather in Kharkov when the cathedral was full of people, but all the people were policemen in disguise.

If you could, as I can, walk along the lines of peasants strung out behind the soldiers or along an entire railway line while the tsar passes by, and hear what these peasants were saying: village elders and peasant policemen rounded up from neighbouring villages and waiting for several days in the cold and slush, without reward and with (only) their bread, for the tsar to pass, you would hear all along the line words totally incompatible with love for autocracy and its representative from the most genuine representatives of the people, the simple peasants. If some 50 years ago in the reign of Nicholas I the prestige of the tsar's authority was still high, during the past 30 years it has continually declined and has recently fallen so low that no one from any class constrains himself any longer from boldly condemning not only the decrees of the government but also the tsar himself, and even swearing at him and laughing at him.

Autocracy is an obsolete form of government which may suit the needs of a people somewhere in Central Africa, cut off from the whole world, but not the needs of the Russian people who are becoming more and more enlightened by the enlightenment common to the whole world. And therefore maintaining this form of government and the Orthodoxy linked with it can only be done as it is now, by means of every kind of violence: a state of emergency, administrative exile, executions, religious persecutions, the banning of books and newspapers, the perversion of education, and, in general, by bad and cruel actions of every type.

Such have been the actions of your reign up to now. Starting with your reply to the Tver deputation which aroused the indignation of all Russian society by calling the most legitimate desires of the people 'foolish day-dreams' – all your decrees about Finland[2] and the seizure of Chinese territories[3], your Hague Conference project[4] accompanied by the strengthening of the army, your weakening of self-government and strengthening of administrative arbitrariness, your support of religious persecutions, your consent to the establishment of a monopoly on spirits, i.e. government traffic in poison for the people, and finally your obstinacy in maintaining corporal punishment despite all the representations made to you for the abolition of this senseless and entirely useless measure, humiliating to the Russian people – all these are actions which you could have avoided taking, had you not set yourself, on the advice of your frivolous aides, an impossible goal – not only to halt the people's life, but to return it to a former obsolete state.

The people can be oppressed by violent measures, but they cannot be governed by them. The only means of effectively governing the people in our time is to head the people's movement from evil to goodness, from darkness to light, and to lead them to the attainment of the goals nearest to it. In order to be able to do this, it is necessary first of all to give the people the opportunity to express their wishes and needs and, having heard these wishes and needs, to fulfil those of them which will answer the needs, not of one class or estate but of the majority, the mass of the working people.

And these wishes which the Russian people will now express, if given the opportunity to do so, will be, in my opinion, the following:

Above all, the working people will say that they wish to be rid of those exclusive laws which place them in the situation of pariahs who do not enjoy the rights of all other citizens; then they will say that they want freedom of movement, freedom of instruction and freedom to profess the religious faith natural to their spiritual needs; and most important, the whole 100 million people will say with one voice that they want freedom to use the land, i.e. the abolition of the right to the private ownership of land.

And this abolition of the right to the private ownership of land is, in my opinion, the nearest goal, the attainment of which the Russian government should set as its task in our time.

In every period of the life of mankind there is a step, appropriate to the time, which comes very close to realising the best forms of life towards which mankind is striving. For Russia fifty years ago the abolition of slavery was such a step. In our time such a step is the liberation of the working masses from the minority which wields power over them – what is called the labour question.

In Western Europe the attainment of this goal is considered possible through the transfer of the factories and workshops to the general use of the workers. Whether such a solution of the question is right or wrong, and whether it is attainable or not by the Western peoples – it is obviously not applicable to Russia as it now is. In Russia, where an enormous part of the population lives on the land and is totally dependent on large-scale landowners, the liberation of the workers obviously cannot be achieved by the transfer of the factories and workshops to the general use. For the Russian people such liberation can be achieved only by abolishing the private ownership of land and by recognising the land as common property – the very thing that has for long been the heartfelt desire of the Russian people, and whose realisation by the Russian government they still look forward to.

I know that these ideas of mine will be taken by your advisers as the height of frivolity and impracticality on the part of a man who has no comprehension at all of the difficulties of governing a state, especially my idea about recognising the land as the common property of the people; but I know too that in order not to be forced to perpetrate more and more cruel violence against the people, there is only one means of action, namely: to make your task the attainment of a goal in advance of the people's wishes, and without waiting for the runaway cart to hit you on the knee, to drive it yourself, i.e. to be in the forefront of achieving the best form of life. For Russia such a goal can only be the abolition of the private ownership of land. Only then can the government be the leader of its people and effectively govern them without making unworthy and forced concessions to the factory workers and students as it does now, and without fearing for its own existence.

Your advisers will tell you that freeing the land from the rights of ownership is a fantasy and an impracticable business. In their opinion, to force a living people of 130 million to cease living or manifesting signs of life, and to squeeze them back into the shell which they long ago outgrew, is not a fantasy and not only not impracticable, but the wisest and most practical course of action. But one only needs to think a bit seriously to understand what really is impracticable, although it is being done, and what on the contrary is not only practicable, but timely and necessary, although it has not yet been begun.

I personally think that in our time the private ownership of land is just as obvious and as crying an injustice as serfdom was 50 years ago. I think that its abolition will place the Russian people on a high level of independence, wellbeing and contentment. I also think that this measure will undoubtedly get rid of all the socialist and revolutionary irritation which is now flaring up among the workers and which threatens the greatest danger both to the people and the government.

But I may be mistaken, and what is more, the solution of this question one way or the other can only be provided by the people themselves if they have an opportunity to express themselves.

In any case, the first business which now faces the government is to eliminate the oppression which prevents the people from expressing their wishes and needs. It is impossible to do good to a man whose mouth we have gagged so as not to hear what he wants for his own good. Only by learning the wishes and needs of all the people, or the majority of them, can one govern the people and do good to them.

Dear brother, you have only one life in this world, and you can waste it agonisingly on vain attempts to halt the movement of mankind, as ordained by God, from evil to goodness, from darkness to light, or you can calmly and joyfully lead it in the service of God and man, by carefully considering the wishes and needs of the people and by dedicating your life to their fulfilment.

However great your responsibility for the years of your reign during which you can do much good or much evil, your responsibility is much greater before God for your life here on which your eternal life depends and which God has given you, not so that you can order evil deeds of all kinds or even be a party to them and allow them, but so that you can carry out His will. His will is not to do evil to people, but good.

Think about this, not in the presence of people, but in the presence of God, and do what God, i.e. your conscience, tells you. And don't be troubled by the obstacles you will encounter if you enter on a new path in life. These obstacles will be eliminated of their own accord and you will not notice them, if only what you do is done not for human glory, but for your own soul, i.e. for God.

Forgive me if I have unwittingly offended or angered you by what I have written in this letter. I was only guided by a desire for the good of the Russian people and of yourself. Whether I have accomplished this will be decided by the future, which I, in all probability, will not see. I have done what I considered my duty[5].

With sincere wishes for your true good,

Your brother,

Lev Tolstoy

Notes.

1. From Le mariage de Figaro, Act III, scene iii.
2. A reference to a manifesto of June 1901 on the obligation of the Finns to do military service in the Russian army.
3. Russia was a party to the partition of China into spheres of influence by the Western powers.
4. A peace conference of the Western powers at The Hague in 1899, called by Russia, but with no tangible results. Tolstoy saw it as an attempt to disguise what he considered to be the militarism of Russian foreign policy.
5. No reply was received to the letter.

Appendix 2

To the Grand Duke Nikolay Mikhaylovich, Gaspra, 7 May 1902.

Dear Nikolay Mikhaylovich,

I received your long and interesting letter the other day. I was very pleased to get it, but certain opinions make me wish to speak my mind about the things over which I disagree with you, and which are particularly dear to me.

First of all, in calling me a great idealist on the basis of the project I am suggesting, you are essentially doing what all the Emperor's advisers who are acquainted with my thought are bound to do, i.e. regard me as a fool who doesn't understand what he's talking about. The attitude towards me of the majority of people, even those well disposed to me, reminds me of a passage from one of Dickens' novels, Hard Times, I think[1], where a clever and serious man, a mechanic, is introduced, who has made a remarkable discovery but who, precisely because he is a very remarkable inventor, is considered by his jolly, good-natured friend to be a person who understands nothing about life and who needs watching like a child in case he should do a lot of very stupid things, and whose words, if he talks about anything outside his own speciality, are received by this good-natured friend with a condescending smile at the naiveta of a person who knows nothing in life except his inventions. The funny side of the situation is that the good-natured friend didn't draw the simple inference that if the mechanic had made important discoveries, he was obviously clever. But if he was clever, it's just as obvious that he wouldn't talk about, and particularly assert, something he didn't know and hadn't thought about.

I feel all the awkwardness and immodesty of this comparison, but I can't refrain from making it, so truly does it show all the falseness of society's attitude in general to the opinions of people who are distinguished in some way from everybody else. This attitude is the more widespread because it absolves people from heeding the meaning of what such people say. 'He's a poet, a mechanic, an idealist', and so there's no point in trying to understand the meaning of what he says. That's the reason why such a strange opinion exists, and even the habit of appointing to posts which require the greatest gifts and intelligence all sorts of Ivanovs, Petrovs, Zengers, Pleves etc., whose only virtue is that they are no different from other people. That's the first point. The second point is that it seems to me – and I regret it very much – that you haven't read and don't know the essence of George's project. The peasant class will not only not oppose the realisation of this project, but will welcome it as the realisation of the wish of many generations of their own class.

The essence of the project surely is that land rent, i.e. the excess value of land as compared with land of the lowest yield, and depending not on man's labour but on nature or the whereabouts of the land, is used for taxes, i.e. for common needs; i.e. the common revenue is used for the common cause. The only effect of this project is that if you own a certain amount of land in Borzhomi and I in the Tula province, nobody takes that land away from me, and I am only obliged to pay a rent for it which is always lower than its yield. I don't know about Borzhomi, but in the Krapiva district of the Tula province the land-rent will be about 5 roubles, while the charge for renting the land now is about 10 roubles, and so the owner of 1,000 desyatins will be obliged to pay the treasury 5,000 roubles and if he is unable to do so, which will probably be the case with 9/10 of landowners, he will give up the land and the peasants, who now pay 10 roubles each to rent it, will obviously be glad to snatch it up for 5 roubles each and will hold it from generation to generation, so that the great mass of the peasantry cannot help but sympathise with this project and will always be in favour of it.

That, in crude outlines, is the essence of Henry George's project. That's the second point. The third point is that the fact that this measure hasn't been carried out either in Europe or America not only doesn't prove that it can't be carried out in Russia, but on the contrary points to the fact that it is only in Russia that it can be carried out, thanks to autocracy. Landowners in Europe and America who make up the greater part of the government will never in their own interests tolerate the freeing of land from the right of private ownership, but even there one can see a movement in this direction, while in Australia and New Zealand this measure is already being realised. Apart from that, this measure is particularly important in our time for the sake of a still agricultural Russia, despite the fact that Witte, Kovalevsky, Mendeleyev and others earnestly wish to direct her on to the path of capitalism and factory production.

That's the third point. Now the fourth point. You write that 'for the realisation of this grandiose idea, a tsar-hero like Peter the Great would be needed, and different collaborators from those whom Nicholas II could have at his disposal'. But I think that no particular heroism is needed for the realisation of this idea, far less the drunken and debauched heroism of Peter the Great, but one only needs the reasonable and honest fulfilment of one's duty as a tsar, in this case most particulary profitable for the tsar himself, i.e. for autocracy, and it seems to me that Nicholas II with his kind heart, as everyone says, could fully realise it, if only he understood its full importance for himself and especially for all his people. As for collaborators, then of course the carrying out of this measure is unthinkable with those bureaucratic corpses, who are all the more corpses the higher they are up the hierarchical ladder of bureaucracy, and all that company such as the Pobedonostsevs, Vannovskys and Chertkovs will have to be removed from any part in the affair. But Russia is full of collaborators who are capable and honest and eager to do a real job which they can love. That's the fourth point.

As for what you say about the need for reforms in all branches of the administration, the pernicious nature of the bureaucracy, the universal passion for profit, all sorts of 'Panamas',[2] excessive militarism, the dissoluteness of morals – all these things will automatically be eliminated from the government milieu as soon as unprincipled people, seeking only their own advancement and profit, are thrown out of it, and people are summoned to the great cause who will love it. And so I not only don't agree with you that the possibility of saving autocracy lies in various patching-up jobs such as the responsibility of ministers (to whom?), or the reformation and revitalising of the highest institutions like the Council of State, the ministries and so on, but, on the contrary, I think that this illusion of the possibility of putting things right by sewing new patches on old rags is the most pernicious of illusions, giving support to that impossible system of things under which we now live. Any such re-formation without the introduction of a higher idea in the name of which people can work with inspiration and self-sacrifice will only be bonnet blanc et blanc bonnet.[3] Generally speaking, the realisation of my idea which seems so unrealisable to you is incomparably more possible than what they are trying to do now – support an obsolete autocracy without any higher idea, but only autocracy for the sake of autocracy.

When I speak about carrying out such a measure by means of the force of authority, I am not speaking from my own point of view whereby I consider any force, even though it seems to us beneficial, to be contrary to the Christian teaching which I profess, but from the point of view of people wishing at all costs to defend an autocracy which is obsolete and pernicious for the autocrat as well as for the people, and to give it the best possible justification.

Forgive me for writing to you at such length about matters over which we can hardly agree, but your letter which touched on problems very dear to me and which have occupied me for a long time roused in me the need to speak my mind. Goodbye; I wish you all the best and thank you once again for carrying out my request. I am not writing to you in my own hand because I have recently had a rechute, not of pneumonia as the doctors say, but of malaria, and I am very weak again.

Yours affectionately,

Lev Tolstoy
Notes.

1. Actually in Little Dorrit, when the mechanical inventor Daniel Doyce is introduced by Mr Meagle with a tale of Doyce's woes at the hands of the Circumlocution Office.
2. A reference to the building of the Panama Canal and the dubious financial transactions connected with it.
3. The equivalent of 'six of one and half a dozen of the other'.

Bibliography

Chapter 1. The final message.
A teacher to the end. A general acknowledgment is due here to all the biographers of Tolstoy hereafter cited.

Chapter 2. The visionary freethinker.
1. Molière. *Le Misanthrope*, act 1, scene 1, lines 157-8.
2. Aylmer Maude. 'Talks with Tolstoy' in *Tolstoy and his problems*. Grant Richards, 1902. (pp. 211-2).
3. Jean-Jacques Rousseau. *Emile* (1762). (p.1, line 1).
4. Raymond A. Dart. *The osteodontokeratic culture of Australopithecus Prometheus*. Pretoria, The Transvaal Museum, 1957
5. John E. Pfeiffer. *The emergence of man*. Nelson, 1970. (p. 172).

Chapter 3. The doctrinal dispute.
1. Leo Tolstoy. 'What I believe' (1884) in Leo Tolstoy. *A confession – The gospel in brief – What I believe*. Oxford University Press, 1940 (The World's Classics). (pp. 370-406).
2. Aylmer Maude. 'Tolstoy's teaching' (1901) in Aylmer Maude. *Tolstoy and his problems*. Grant Richards, 1902. (p. 27).
3. Aylmer Maude. 'Talks with Tolstoy' in Aylmer Maude. *Tolstoy and his problems*. Grant Richards, 1902. (pp. 192-3).
4. Matthew Arnold. *Literature and dogma*. Smith, Elder & Co, 1873. *God and the Bible*. Smith, Elder & Co, 1874.
5. Matthew Arnold. 'Count Leo Tolstoi' in Matthew Arnold. *Essays in criticism*. Dent, 1964 (Everyman's Library). (p. 371).
6. A.N. Wilson. *Tolstoy*. Hamish Hamilton, 1988. (p. 326).
7. A.N. Wilson. *Against religion*. Chatto & Windus, 1991.
8. E.B. Greenwood. *Tolstoy:* the comprehensive vision. Dent, 1975. (p. 121).
9. Blaise Pascal. *Pensées*. Dent, 1913 (Collection Gallia). (p. 105) (L. Brunschvig, III, 233).
10. Leo Tolstoy. 'The Kingdom of God is within you' (1893) in Leo Tolstoy. *The Kingdom of God and Peace essays*. Oxford University Press, 1936 (The World's Classics). (p. 42).

Chapter 4. The critical foul.
1. Tatyana Tolstoy. *Tolstoy remembered*. Michael Joseph, 1977. (p. 35).
2. Ibid. (pp. 116-7).
3. Henri Troyat. *Tolstoy*. Penguin Books, 1970 (Pelican Biographies). (pp. 290-1).

Chapter 5. Violent birth of the State.
General acknowledgments for the factual information in this chapter are due to: *Encyclopaedia Britannica,* 11th edition, 1910-1911. Article 'Russia'. Christopher Hill. *Lenin and the Russian revolution.* Hodder & Stoughton Ltd, 1947. (Teach Yourself History Library; ed. A.L. Rowse).

Chapter 6. Violent life of the State.
1. Leo Tolstoy. *Sevastopol in December 1854., Sevastopol in May 1855. Sevastopol in August 1855.*
2. Henri Troyat. *Tolstoy* (1965). Penguin Books Ltd., 1970. (Pelican Biographies). (p. 235).
3. Aylmer Maude. 'War and patriotism' in Aylmer Maude. *Tolstoy and his problems.* Grant Richards, 1902. (pp. 182-3).
4. Parker Thomas Moon. *Imperialism and world politics.* New York, Macmillan, 1926.
5. Leo Tolstoy. 'Bethink yourselves!' (1904) in Leo Tolstoy. *Recollections and essays.* Oxford University Press, 1937 (Tolstoy Centenary Edition). (p. 245). (Emphasis added).
6. Ibid. (p. 255). (Emphasis added). 7. Ibid. (p. 263). (Emphasis added).
8. Leo Tolstoy. 'The Kingdom of God is within you' (1893) in Leo Tolstoy. *The Kingdom of God and Peace essays.* Oxford University Press, 1936 (The World's Classics). (pp. 334-401).
9. V.I. Lenin. 'Lev Tolstoi as the mirror of the Russian revolution' in *Articles on Tolstoi.* Moscow, Progress Publishers, 1971. (p. 6).
10. Etienne de la Boétie. Discours de la servitude volontaire (1548). Paris, Flammarion, 1983. (p. 136).
11. Leo Tolstoy. *The law of love and the law of violence.* Anthony Blond, 1948. (pp. 33-5).
12. Henri Troyat. Op. Cit (pp. 314-6).
13 Walter Kerr. *The Shabunin affair: an episode in the life of Leo Tolstoy.* Ithaca and London, Cornell University Press, 1982.

Chapter 7. The verdict of history.
1. Parker Thomas Moon. *Imperialism and world politics.* New York, Macmillan, 1926. (pp. 173-4).
2. Ibid. (p. 174).
3. Ibid. (pp. 177-8). (Emphasis added).
4. Ibid. (p. 179). (Emphasis added).
5. Ibid. (p. 169). (Emphasis added).
6. G.P. Gooch. *History of our time.* Oxford University Press, 1946. (Home University Library of Modern Knowledge). (pp. 75-6).
7. Anatole France. *L'Ile des pingouins.* Paris, Calmann-Lavy, 1908. (p. 63). – . *Penguin Island;* translated by A.W. Evans. Watts & Co., 1931. (The Thinker's Library, No. 21). (p. 35).

Chapter 8. Tolstoy on the State: the critical assessment.
1. Henry David Thoreau. *Civil disobedience* in Henry David Thoreau. *Walden and Civil disobedience.* Penguin Books, 1986.

(Penguin Classics). (p. 385). (New York, Holt, Rinehart and Winston, 1948) (p. 281).

2. Aylmer Maude. Introduction to "The Slavery of our times" in Aylmer Maude. *Tolstoy and his problems*. Grant Richards, 1902. (p. 105).

3. *Ibid*. (p. 105).

4. *Ibid*. (p. 105).

5. Aylmer Maude. 'The Tsar's coronation' in Aylmer Maude. *Tolstoy and his problems*. Grant Richards, 1902. (p. 111).

6. Aylmer Maude. *The Life of Tolstoy,* vol.1, first fifty years. Oxford University Press, 1987. (p. 239).

7. *Ibid*. (pp. 239-40).

8. Jean-Jacques Rousseau. *Du Contrat social* (1762). Manchester University Press, 1918. (English version – *The Social contract and Discourses;* translated by G.D.H. Cole. Dent, 1915. (Everyman's Library).

9. V.I. Lenin. 'Tolstoi and the proletarian struggle' in V.I. Lenin. *Articles on Tolstoi*. Moscow, Progress Publishers, 1951. (p. 21).

10. Victor Shklovsky. *Lev Tolstoy*. Moscow, Progress Publishers, 1978. (p. 552).

11. *Ibid*. (p. 691).

12. Ernest J. Simmons. *Tolstoy*. Routledge & Kegan Paul, 1973. (Routledge Author Guides). (p. 174).

13. *Ibid*. (p. 208).

14. *Ibid*. (p. 209).

15. Henri Troyat. *Tolstoy*. Penguin Books, 1970. (Pelican Biographies). (p. 637).

16. Theodore Redpath. *Tolstoy*. Bowes & Bowes, 1960. (p. 29). 17. A.N. Wilson. *Tolstoy*. Hamish Hamilton, 1988. (p. 101).

18. *Ibid*. (p. 331).

19. Leo Tolstoy. *'The Kingdom of God is within you'* (1893) in Leo Tolstoy. *The Kingdom of God and Peace essays*. Oxford University Press, 1936 (The World's Classics). (p. 283). (Emphasis added).

Chapter 9. The Golden Regiment.

1. Leo Tolstoy. *What then must we do?* (1886). Oxford University Press, 1925. (The World's Classics). (Ch.1).

2. Leo Tolstoy. 'Boyhood' (1854) in Leo Tolstoy. *Childhood, Boyhood, Youth*. Penguin Books, 1964. (Penguin Classics). (p. 119).

3. Leo Tolstoy. *What then must we do?* (1886). Oxford University Press, 1925. (The World's Classics). (p. 73).

4. Adam Smith. *An inquiry into the nature and causes of the wealth of nations* (1776). Henry Frowde, 1904. (The World's Classics).

5. Leo Tolstoy. *Anna Karenina* (1878). Penguin Books, 1954. (Penguin Classics). (p. 711). (Emphasis added).

Chapter 10. Quest for the 'green stick'.

1. Henri Troyat. *Tolstoy*. Penguin Books, 1970. (Pelican Biographies). (pp. 200-1).

2. Henry George. *Social problems* (1883). New York, Robert Schalkenbach Foundation, 1934.
3. Leo Tolstoy. *What then must we do?* (1886). Oxford University Press, 1925. (The World's Classics). (p. 311).
4. *Ibid.* (p. 338).
5. Henry George. *The science of political economy* (1897). New York, Robert Schalkenbach Foundation, 1968. (p. 332).
6. *Encyclopaedia Britannica,* 11th edition, 1910-11, article 'Russia'.
7. Henry George. *Protection or free trade* (1886). New York, Robert Schalkenbach Foundation, 1980. (p. 68).
8. Matthew Arnold. 'Count Leo Tolstoi (1887)' in Matthew Arnold. *Essays in criticism.* Dent, 1964. (Everyman's Library). (p. 372).
9. Matthew Arnold. *Culture and anarchy* (1869). Nelson, n.d.. 10. Henry George. *Progress and poverty* (1879). Dent, n.d. (Everyman's Library).
10. Leo Tolstoy. *What then must we do?* (1886). Oxford University Press, 1935. (The World's Classics). (pp. 166-7).

Chapter 11. The Single Tax.
1. Aylmer Maude. 'Talks with Tolstoy' in Aylmer Maude. *Tolstoy and his problems.* Grant Richards, 1902. (pp. 204-5). (Emphasis added).
2. Henry George jr. *The life of Henry George.* New York, Robert Schalkenbach Foundation, 1960. (p. 34).
3. Henry George. *Progress and poverty* (1879). Dent, n.d. (Everyman's Library). (Bk.v, ch.ii – p. 208).
4. Henry George jr. *The life of Henry George.* New York, Robert Schalkenbach Foundation, 1960. (pp. 178-9).
5. *Ibid.* (p. 210).
6. Henry George. *Progress and poverty* (1879). Dent, n.d. (Everyman's Library). (Bk.i, ch.i – p.15).
7. *Ibid.* (Bk.viii, ch.iv – p. 301).
8. *Ibid.* (Bk.iii, ch.ii – p. 121).
9. Henry George. *Why the landowner cannot shift the tax on land values* (an editorial reprinted from *The Standard).* New York, Robert Schalkenbach Foundation, n.d. (p. 4).

Chapter 12. Tolstoy on Henry George.
1. Henry George. *Social problems* (1883). New York, Robert Schalkenbach Foundation, 1981. (p. 242).
2. Leo Tolstoy. *Tolstoy's letters;* ed. R.F. Christian. London University, The Athlone Press, 1978. (p. 512).
3. Leo Tolstoy. *Tolstoy's diaries;* ed. R.F. Christian. London University, The Athlone Press, 1985. (p. 337).
4. Henry George. *A perplexed philosopher* (1892). Henry George Foundation of Great Britain, 1937.
5. Henry George. *Progress and poverty* (1879). Dent, n.d. (Everyman's Library). (Bk.viii, ch.ii – p. 288).
6. Leo Tolstoy. 'Letters on Henry George' in *Recollections and*

185

essays. Oxford University Press, 1937. (Tolstoy Centenary
Edition). (p. 189).
7. Leo Tolstoy. *Tolstoy's diaries;* ed. R.F. Christian. London
University, The Athlone Press, 1985. (p. 409).
8. Leo Tolstoy. *Resurrection* (1899). Oxford University Press, 1916.
(The World's Classics).
9. Leo Tolstoy. *The slavery of our times* (1900). The Porcupine Press,
1958. (p. 40).
10. *Ibid.* (p. vii).
11. Leo Tolstoy. *Tolstoy's letters;* ed. R.F. Christian. London
University, The Athlone Press, 1978. (p. 615).
12. Leo Tolstoy. *Tolstoy's diaries;* ed. R.F. Cbristian. London
University, The Athlone Press, 1985. (p. 537).
13. Henry George. *The Crime of poverty*. New York, Robert
Schalkenbach Foundation, n.d.
14. Leo Tolstoy. 'A great iniquity' in Leo Tolstoy. *Recollections and
essays*. Oxford University Press, 1937. (Tolstoy Centenary
Edition). (pp. 285-6).
15. Leo Tolstoy. *Tolstoy's diaries;* ed. R.F. Christian. London
University, The Athlone Press, 1985. (p. 552).
16. *Ibid.* (p. 553).
17. *Ibid.* (p. 556).
18. *Ibid.* (p. 556).
19. *Ibid.* (p. 614).
20. *Ibid.* (p. 617).
21. *Ibid.* (p. 617).
22. *Ibid.* (p. 627).
23. *Ibid.* (p. 629).
24. *Ibid.* (p. 637).
25. *Ibid.* (p. 639).
26. Leo Tolstoy. *Tolstoy on land and slavery*. Land Values
Publication Department (376-7, The Strand, London), n.d. (p. 68).
27. *Ibid.* (p. 70-1).

Chapter 13. Were they socialists?.
1. Aylmer Maude. 'Talks with Tolstoy' in Aylmer Maude. *Tolstoy
and his problems*. Grant Richards, 1902. (p. 204)
2. *Encyclopaedia Britannica,* 11th edition, 1910-11, article
'Socialism'. (Emphasis added).
3. Henry George. *Social problems* (1883). New York, Robert
Schalkenbach Foundation, 1981. (pp. 176-7).
4. Leo Tolstoy. *The slavery of our times*. The Porcupine Press, 1958.
(p. 49).
5. Henry George. *Progress and poverty* (1879). Dent, n.d.
(Everyman's Library). (Bk.vi, ch.i – p. 228).
6. Henry George. *The condition of labour:* an open letter to Pope Leo
XIII (1891). Land & Liberty Press Ltd., 1947. (pp. 55-6).
7. *Ibid.* (p. 56).
8. *Ibid.* (pp. 52-3).

9. Karl Marx. 'Criticism of the Gotha programme of the Social Democratic Party of Germany (1875)', reprinted in the *International Socialist Review*, May 1908.
10. Karl Marx. *Capital, vol.3;* tr. E. and C. Paul. Allen & Unwin, 1928. (p. 732).
11. Karl Marx and Friedrich Engels. *The communist manifesto.* Penguin Books, 1967. (p. 104).

Chapter 14. Critics of Tolstoy's Georgism.
1. Leo Tolstoy. 'What is art?' (1898) in Leo Tolstoy. *What is art? and Essays on art.* Oxford University Press, 1930 (The World's Classics). (p. 123).
2. Aylmer Maude. 'Tolstoy's view of art' (1900) in Aylmer Maude. *Tolstoy and his problems.* Grant Richards, 1902. (pp. 66-7). (Emphasis added).
3. Henri Troyat. *Tolstoy.* Penguin Books, 1967 (Pelican Biographies). (p. 757).
4. *Ibid.* (p. 796).
5. A.N. Wilson. Tolstoy. Hamish Hamilton, 1988. (p. 476).
6. *Ibid.* (p. 495).
7. Henry George. *Progress and poverty* (1879). Dent, n.d. (Everyman's Library). (Bk. vi, ch. ii – p. 234).
8. E.J. Simmons. Tolstoy. Routledge & Kegan Paul, 1973 (Routledge Author Guides). (p. 216).
9. Theodore Redpath. Tolstoy. Bowes & Bowes, 1960 (Studies in Modern European Literature and Thought). (pp. 82-3).
10. Victor Shklovsky. *Lev Tolstoy.* Moscow, Progress Publishers, 1978. (p. 690).
11. *Ibid.* (p. 698).
12. Henry George. *Progress and poverty* (1879). Dent, n.d. (Everyman's Library). (Bk. vi, ch. i – pp. 231-2).
13. Victor Shklovsky. *Lev Tolstoy.* Moscow, Progress Publishers, 1978. (p. 691).
14. Henry Gifford. Tolstoy. Oxford University Press, 1982 (Past Masters). (pp. 56-7).
15. Aylmer Maude. 'Talks with Tolstoy' in Aylmer Maude. *Tolstoy and his problems.* Grant Richards, 1902.
16. Aylmer Maude. *The Life of Tolstoy.* Oxford University Press, 1987. (vol. ii – p. 328).
17. Henry George. *Progress and poverty* (1879). Dent, n.d. (Everyman's Library). (Bk. viii, ch. ii – p. 288).
18. Aylmer Maude. *The Life of Tolstoy.* Oxford University Press, 1987. (vol. ii – pp. 340-1). (Emphasis added).
19. Victor Shklovsky. Lev Tolstoy. Moscow, Progress Publishers, 1978. (p. 775).

Chapter 15. Land value taxation in action.
1. Roy Douglas. *Land, people and politics.* Allison & Busby, 1976.
2. *Liberal Magazine,* 1912: 618. See also Randolph S. Churchill.

Winston Churchill, vol.2, young statesman, 1901-1914.
Heinemann, 1967. (pp. 323-4).

3. Marvin Swartz. 'A study in futility: the British radicals at the outbreak of the First World War' in A.J.A. Morris ed. *Edwardian radicalism.* Routledge & Kegan Paul, 1974. (p. 247).

4. *Local authority statistics, 1985-86.* New Zealand Department of Statistics, 1988.

5. Steven B. Cord. *The evidence for land value taxation.* Center for the Study of Economics (2000 Century Plaza – Suite 238, Columbia MD 21044, U.S.A.), 1987.

6. *Affordable housing: a missing link.* Kensington MD, Center for Public Dialogue (10615, Brunswick Avenue, Kensington, Maryland 20895, U.S.A.), 1988. (p. 1).

7. Henry George. *Protection or free trade* (1885). New York, Robert Schalkenbach Foundation, 1980.

8. Aylmer Maude. 'Talks with Tolstoy' in Aylmer Maude. *Tolstoy and his problems.* Grant Richards, 1902. (pp. 210-1). (Emphasis added).

9. *Incentive taxation, December 1987.* Center for the Study of Economics (2000 Century Plaza – Suite 238, Columbia, Maryland 21044, U.S.A.).

10. Steven B. Cord. Catalyst. Indiana Pa, Henry George Foundation of America (580 North Sixth Street, Indiana, Pennsylvania 15701), 1979. (pp. 32-3).

Chapter 16. War: the useless remedies.

1. Leo Tolstoy. 'Bethink yourselves!' in Leo Tolstoy. *Recollections and essays.* Oxford University Press, 1937 (Tolstoy Centenary Edition). (pp. 225-6).

2. Henri Troyat. *Tolstoy.* Penguin Books, 1970 (Pelican Biographies). (pp. 655-6).

3. Sidney Bradshaw Fay. *The origins of the World War, 2nd ed.* New York, Macmillan, 1936. 2 vols. in 1. (vol. i – pp. 277-293).

4. Parker Thomas Moon. *Imperialism and world politics.* New York, Macmillan, 1926. (p. 274).

5. Erich Maria Remarque. *All quiet on the western front;* tr. A.W. Wheen. Putnam, 1929. (pp. 212-3). (Emphasis added).

6. *Echo de Paris,* 21st July 1935.

Chapter 17. Towards the precipice.

1. Leo Tolstoy. 'The Kingdom of God is within you' (1893) in Leo Tolstoy. *The Kingdom of God and Peace essays.* Oxford University Press, 1936 (The World's Classics). (pp. 281-2).

2. Leo Tolstoy. 'Introduction to a short biography of William Lloyd Garrison' in Leo Tolstoy. *The Kingdom of God and Peace essays.* Oxford University Press, 1936 (The World's Classics). (p. 580).

3. Leo Tolstoy. 'The Kingdom of God is within you' (1893) in Leo Tolstoy. *The Kingdom of God and Peace essays.* Oxford University Press, 1936 (The World's Classics). (p. 288).

4. *Arming Saddam: the supply of British military equipment to Iraq, 1979-1990.* Campaign Against Arms Trade (11, Goodwin Street, Finsbury Park, London N4 3HQ), 1991.

5. *Hansard,* 14th December 1989.

General acknowledgments are due also to: *Death on delivery: the impact of the arms trade on the Third World.* Campaign Against Arms Trade (11, Goodwin Street, Finsbury Park, London N4 3HQ), 1989. *Encyclopedia Britannica,* 15th edition. Article 'Iraq'. Parker Thomas Moon. *Imperialism and world politics.* New York, Macmillan, 1926.

Chapter 18. Tolstoy and *perestroika.*

1. Albert Jay Nock. *Our enemy the State.* Caldwell, Idaho, The Caxton Printers Ltd., 1935.

2. Mihkail Gorbachev. *Perestroika:* new thinking for our country and the world. Collins, 1987. (p.23). (Emphasis added).

3. Konstantin Simis. U.S.S.R.: secrets of a corrupt society. Dent, 1982. (p.35).

4. B.P. Pockney. 'Perestroika versus the military-industrial complex'. 19th International Conference, International Union for Land Value Taxation and Free Trade, London, 21-27 March 1991.

5. Eduard Shevardnadze. *The future belongs to freedom.* Sinclair-Stevenson, 1991.

6. Mikhail Gorbachev. *Perestroika: new thinking for our country and the world.* Collins, 1987. (pp.27-36).

7. *Ibid.* (p.97). (Emphasis added).

8. Richard Noyes. *Now the synthesis: capitalism, socialism and the new social contract.* London, Shepheard-Walwyn (New York, Holmes & Meier), 1991. (p. 225).

9. Ian Barron. 'Georgists' mission to U.S.S.R. is successful' in *Land & Liberty,* July/August 1991.

10. Penny Symon. ' "Preservation of Union is key", says Gorbachev' in *The Daily Telegraph,* 1 January 1991.

11. 'Raising the last Iron Curtain' in *Soviet Weekly,* 7 November 1991.

12. *Law of the Russian Soviet Federated Socialist Republic on revenue from land,* Section 1, Article 3. 11 October 1991.

13 Mark Frankland, *"Lipstick-deep revolution holds kiss of death",* The Observer, London, December 9, 1990. In a letter sent to Stolypin's ministry on July 26, 1907, Tolstoy described private land ownership as "the oldest and greatest injustice of all, which is common to all places: the individual ownership of land".

14 Jonathan Steele, *"Russia allows private land",* The Guardian, London, December 4, 1990.

15 John Lloyd, "Yeltsin presses Congress for wider powers", The Financial Times, London, April 22, 1992.

16 See, for example, the summary of work carried out inside the OECD, in an article by Ferdinand Kuba, *"Restructuring Soviet Agriculture",* The OECD Observer, February/March 1992, which (on p.174) refers to "such crucial issues as...private ownership of

agricultural land".

17 Such a strategy is elaborated in Fred Harrison, *"Post-socialism and the Single Tax: a holistic philosophy"*, in Richard Noyes (editor), Capitalism, Socialism and the New Social Contract, London: Shepheard Walwyn/New York: Holmes & Meier, 1991.

18 P. Jurkovic, professor of economics at the University of Zagreb – in Yugoslavia, an associate member of the OECD – in The Role of Tax Reform in Central and Eastern European Economies, Paris: OECD, 1991, p.49. Prof. Jurkovic insists on uniformity of misery: "Relying on the experience of developed countries means that central and east European countries must take over from the west the basic types of taxes, such as personal income tax, corporation tax, sales tax and contributions for social security, and the basic principles on which they were formed.". *Ibid., p.28.* Italics added. "For social security, and the basic principles on which they were formed.". *Ibid., p.28.* Italics added.

Index

195